I0190685

CHRIST EVANGELICAL BIBLE INSTITUTE

The Threeness of God

Rev. Joseph Adam Pearson, Ph.D.

Copyright

Copyright © 2023 by Rev. Joseph Adam Pearson, Ph.D.

This work is a revision of an earlier version copyrighted by the United States Copyright Office:

Copyright 2021 (TX-009-046-464)
Copyright 2020 (TX-008-971-643)

All rights reserved.

Paper Book Identifier:

ISBN-13: 9781734294729

Published by
Christ Evangelical Bible Institute
(SAN: 920-3753)

Last edited on January 3, 2023
Dayton, Tennessee

Dedication

This short work is dedicated to the human beings who will be alive when the *only-begotten* Son of God, Christ Jesus, returns to Earth for his Millennial reign of peace. By then, this world will have lost at least one-half of its population from warfare, lawlessness, anarchy, global warming, famine, drought, pestilence, plague, cataclysmic disaster, and the harvesting of wicked people (i.e., their removal from Earth) by the reaper-angels of God.

Notes

As used in this book, *KJV* is an abbreviation for the public domain *King James Version* of the Holy Bible. To ensure their accuracy throughout this book, all paraphrases of the public domain *King James Version* of the Holy Bible were finalized only after first checking: (1) the Masoretic Hebrew text of the Tanakh (the Jewish Bible) for accuracy of passages from the *KJV Old Testament* and (2) the earliest Greek text extant for accuracy of passages from the *KJV New Testament*. Additionally, to enhance readability of the public domain *KJV* text, archaic English words like *hath, thou,* and *ye* have been changed to their modern equivalents.

Most transliterated Hebrew and Greek words referenced within the text of this book are noted by their respective numbers [in brackets with a preceding "H" for Hebrew or "G" for Greek] from the *Dictionary of the Hebrew Bible* and the *Dictionary of the Greek Bible* found in *Strong's Exhaustive Concordance of the Bible* by James Strong (Copyright 1890), Crusade Bible Publishers, Inc., Nashville.

Although God the Father (i.e., the *LORD God Almighty)* and God the Son (i.e., the *Lord Jesus Christ)* are consubstantially united in the Godhead along with God the Holy Spirit, in order to distinguish *God the Father* from *God the Son* in this book, an upper case "H" is used for personal pronouns specifically referring to *God the Father (He, His,* and *Him)* and a lower case "h" is used for personal pronouns specifically referring to *God the Son (he, his,* and *him).*

Clarification: The word *consubstantial* — meaning "having the same nature and essence and, therefore, made of the same substance" — has been translated from ὁμοούσιον *(homoousion),* the accusative case form of the Greek word ὁμοούσιος *(homoousios).* The word *co-essential* is also translated from the Greek word ὁμοούσιος *(homoousios)* and has two different senses, imports, or significations:

(1) "of equal importance" *(meaning a)* as well as (2) "having the same nature and essence and, therefore, made of the same substance" *(meaning b).* In relation to the Godhead, *nature, substance,* and *essence* denote Spirit (i.e., the nature, substance, or essence of the Supreme Being) and are used synonymously in this book; they describe *spiritual/invisible nature, spiritual/invisible substance,* and *spiritual/invisible essence* — in contrast to words that describe *physicality, materiality, corporeality, matter,* and *physical energy.*

Whenever the word *God* is used in this book (i.e., with an upper case "G"), the reader should assume that the word is referring to the God of the Holy Bible — who is the *LORD God Almighty* or *Yahweh* (YHWH), the one true and only real Creator-God.

Although the Creator-God does not possess a human gender, there are no apologies for the use of the male pronouns *He, His, and Him* in this book when referring to the LORD God Almighty *(God the Father)* for the following reasons: In general, certain words in theology and philosophy are capitalized to show that they represent qualities and characteristics that transcend human understanding and experience. This includes the pronouns *He, His,* and *Him* and even the word *God* itself. *She* and *Her* are not used in this book when referring to the Creator-God because many people in the early 21st century, if not most people, have a tendency to confuse the use of female pronouns with advocating Wicca and other ancient and modern pagan cults that worship the Mother-Goddess — such as those devoted to Cybele, Aphrodite (Venus), Hecate, Artemis (Diana), Magna Mater, Ma, Anaitis, Ashtoreth (Astarte), Ma'at, Morrigan, etc.

For the sake of clarity, when the author of *The Threeness of God* uses the phrase *the present author,* he is referring to himself.

Table of Contents

1. Threeness and Oneness

The title of this book is *The Threeness of God* rather than *The Trinity of God* or *The Tri-unity of God* because this book has been written to help those Christians who are confused by other Christians who refer to themselves and their doctrines as *Oneness.*

Formally, the *Threeness of God* can be referred to as *Trinitarianism* and its adherents as *trinitarians,* and the *Oneness of God* can be referred to as *Unitarianism* and its adherents as *unitarians* (not to be confused with the adherents of Unitarian Universalism, which religion is neither a mainstream *Oneness* nor even a Christian denomination).

Although the present author cannot speak for all *Threeness* adherents, they believe — generally speaking — that the one Supreme Being (i.e., *the Divinity* or *the Godhead*) is partitioned into coequal, coeternal, consubstantial, co-essential, and simultaneously-existing parts, or *persons,* known as *God the Father, God the Son,* and *God the Holy Spirit.* And, although the present author cannot speak for all *Oneness* adherents, they believe — generally speaking — that the one Supreme Being (i.e., *the Divinity* or *the Godhead*) manifested Himself sequentially in three successive ages, or dispensations, as *Father, Son,* and *Holy Spirit* (with the phrase *Holy Ghost* often preferred by them over *Holy Spirit*).

Author's Note: A *Twoness of God* perspective also exists. Formally referred to as *Binitarianism,* binitarian adherents — generally speaking — separate the Divinity into *God the Father* and *God the Son,* recognizing *the Holy Spirit* as the force, power, and essence of the entire Godhead.

Having received salvation at the age of eight in a Trinitarian denominational church, the present author was clearly taught, easily understood, and readily accepted the doctrines associated with *the Threeness of God.* It was not until the present author was approximately forty-five years of age that he was introduced to a *Oneness* perspective. (I am seventy-four now.)

Because the present author did not understand why *Oneness* adherents separate themselves from *Threeness* adherents, he asked God the Father to explain it to him in terms simple enough for him to understand as well as for him to share with others. God the Holy Spirit responded to this request in His still, small voice, saying:

> Some of My people emphasize the *Three* in *Three-in-one,* and some of My people emphasize the *One* in *three-in-One.* Either position is acceptable to Me provided that no one worships any created being [either spiritual or natural] and that they worship only Me.

Author's Note: Regardless of *Threeness* or *Oneness* perspectives, Jesus Christ, Christ Jesus, or Jesus the Christ is *not* considered a created being by either perspective in mainstream Christianity. In fact, it is considered heresy by adherents of either *Threeness* or *Oneness* perspectives to present Jesus Christ as a created being. Based on the Holy Bible, Jesus Christ is considered the Word of God, the Logos, the Lamb of God, the only-begotten Son of God, and God-Incarnate — that is, God "manifested in the flesh" *(1 Timothy 3:16 KJV)* — but *not* a created being.

It is the present author's perspective, based on his experiences with *Oneness* adherents, that they have made their doctrines inferior to those of *Threeness:* (1) by arrogantly believing that their doctrinal position is superior to the *Threeness* doctrinal position; (2) by not embracing the fullness of the Godhead; (3) by their inability to conceptualize the Godhead in three co-, synchronously-, or simultaneously-existing persons; and (4) by accepting collateral doctrinal errors like (a) forced *speaking in tongues* and (b) *material prosperity* for all Christians.

To be sure, it did not have to be this way. The *Oneness* perspective did not have to develop in competition with the *Threeness* perspective. *Oneness* adherents could have simply decided to emphasize the true unity of God at the same time that they maintained a healthy fellowship with other mainstream Christians. Instead, they chose to emphasize certain verses in Scripture and ignore or misinterpret other verses. Some even chose, and still choose, to view the *Threeness* position as blasphemous, antichrist, polytheistic, and less than *full gospel.*

Examples of Bible verses that are used to support a *Oneness* perspective include verses found in the Old Testament as well as the New Testament, *such as:*

Hear, O Israel: The LORD our God is one LORD. *Deuteronomy 6:4 KJV*

[Christ Jesus said:] "I and My Father are one." *John 10:30 KJV*

That God the Father and God the Son have one *Being* means that they are partitioned parts of one another that together function as a whole, much like one human brain has multiple lobes that together function as a whole even though they each have a different morphology, location, purpose, function, and role. If *Oneness* reasoning were taken to a logical, albeit inaccurate, extreme, it could easily conclude and assert that, eventually, the Creator-God and the saved souls of created beings would be indistinguishable from one another in response to this prayer of Jesus Christ:

{20} "Neither pray I for these alone, but for them also which shall believe on me through their word [or testimony]; {21} That they all may be one; as You, Father, are in me, and I in You, that they also may be one in us: that the world may believe that You have *sent* me. {22} And the glory which You gave to me I have given to them; that they may be one, even as we [Father and Son] are one: {23} I in them, and You in me, that they may be

11

made perfect in one; and that the world may know that You have *sent* me, and have loved them, as You have loved me." *John 17:20-23 KJV (Paraphrase)*

Author's Note: "That they may be one" in John 17:21, 22, and 23 is an illustration of figurative language with metaphysical meaning, representing union of purpose for saved souls as integrated members of the Body of Christ, who are not indistinguishably *one.*

2. The *One Sent*

The New Testament is clear that Jesus Christ was *sent.* If someone is *sent,* the one *sent* has not *sent* himself; the one *sent* is *sent* by someone else. The *Oneness* perspective has God the Father showing up on Earth as God the Son. However, Scripture makes itself clear in the following verses that it was God the Father who *sent* God the Son (the present author has placed each *sent* in italics in the following direct quotes from Jesus Christ):

"He who receives you [the twelve disciples] receives me [God the Son], and he who receives me receives Him [God the Father] who *sent* me." *Matthew 10:40 KJV*

"He who hears you hears me [God the Son]; and he who despises you despises me; and he who despises me despises Him [God the Father] who *sent* me." *Luke 10:16 KJV*

"For God [the Father] *sent* not His Son into the world to condemn the world; but that the world through him might be saved." *John 3:17 KJV*

Jesus said unto them, "My meat [the heart, or substance, of what I do] is to do the will of Him who *sent* me, and to finish His work." *John 4:34 KJV*

{23} "All men should honor the Son even as they honor the Father. He who honors not the Son honors not the Father who has *sent* him. {24} Truly, truly, I say to you: he who hears my word, and believes on Him who *sent* me, has everlasting life, and shall not come into condemnation; but is passed from death unto life." *John 5:23-24 KJV*

"I can of my own self do nothing: as I hear, I judge: and my judgment is just; because I seek not my own will but the will of the Father who has *sent* me." *John 5:30 KJV*

"But I have greater witness than that of John: for the works that the Father has given me to finish (the same works that I do) bear witness of me, that the Father has *sent* me." *John 5:36 KJV*

{37} "And the Father Himself, who has *sent* me, has borne witness of me. You have neither heard His voice at any time nor seen His shape. {38} And you do not have His word abiding in you: because the one whom He has *sent*, him you believe not." *John 5:37-38 KJV*

Jesus answered and said unto them, "This is the work of God, that you believe on him whom He has *sent*." *John 6:29 KJV*

{38} "For I came down from heaven, not to do my own will, but the will of Him that *sent* me. {39} And this is the Father's will who has *sent* me, that of all which He has given me I should lose nothing, but should raise it up again at the last day. {40} And this is the will of Him that *sent* me, that everyone who sees the Son, and believes on him, may have everlasting life: and I will raise him up at the last day." *John 6:38-40 KJV*

"No man can come to me unless the Father that *sent* me draw him: and I will raise him up at the last day." *John 6:44 KJV*

"As the living Father has *sent* me, and I live by the Father: so he that [experiences] me, even he shall live by me." *John 6:57 KJV*

Jesus answered them, and said, "My doctrine is not mine, but His that *sent* me." *John 7:16 KJV*

"He that speaks of himself seeks his own glory: but he that seeks His glory that *sent* him, the same is true, and no unrighteousness is in him." *John 7:18 KJV*

{28} Then cried Jesus in the temple as he taught, saying, "You both know me and know where I am from: and I am not come of myself, but He that *sent* me is true, whom you know not. {29} But I know Him: for I am from Him, and He has *sent* me." {33} Then said Jesus to them, "Yet a little while am I with you, and then I go to Him that *sent* me." *John 7:28-29, 33 KJV*

{16} "If I judge, my judgment is true: for I am not alone, but I and the Father that *sent* me." {18} "I am one that bear witness of myself, and the Father that *sent* me bears witness of me." *John 8:16, 18 KJV*

{26} "I have many things to say and to judge of you: but He that *sent* me is true; and I speak to the world those things which I have heard from Him." {29} "And He that *sent* me is with me: the Father has not left me alone; for I always do those things that please Him." *John 8:26, 29 KJV*

Jesus said to them, "If God were your Father, you would love me: for I proceeded forth and came from God; neither came I of myself, but He *sent* me." *John 8:42 KJV*

"I must work the works of Him that *sent* me while it is day: the night comes when no man can work." *John 9:4 KJV*

"Say you of him, whom the Father has sanctified and *sent* into the world, 'You blaspheme!' because I said, 'I am the Son of God?'" *John 10:36 KJV*

{41b} And Jesus lifted up his eyes, and said, "Father, I thank You that You have heard me. {42} And I knew that You hear me always: but because of the people who stand by me I said it, that they may believe that You have *sent* me." *John 11:41b-42 KJV*

{44} Jesus cried and said, "Whoever believes on me, believes not on me, but on Him that *sent* me. {45} And he that sees me sees Him that *sent* me. {49} For I have not spoken of myself; but the Father which *sent* me, He gave me a commandment, what I should say, and what I should speak." *John 12:44-45,49 KJV*

Author's Note: *Oneness adherents* who claim John 12:45 as indicative that God the Father *is* God the Son are not recognizing that "he who sees me sees Him that *sent* me" is figurative language with metaphysical meaning and not literal language with physical meaning.

"Truly, truly, I say unto you, 'The servant is not greater than his lord; neither he that is *sent* greater than He that *sent* him.'" *John 13:16 KJV*

"Verily, verily, I say unto you, 'He that receives whomever I send receives me; and whoever that receives me receives Him that *sent* me.'" *John 13:20 KJV*

"Whoever that does not love me will not keep my sayings: and the word that you hear from me is not mine, but the Father's which *sent* me." *John 14:24 KJV*

"But all these things will they do to you for my name's sake, because they do not know Him that *sent* me." *John 15:21 KJV*

"But now I go my way to Him that *sent* me; and none of you ask me, 'Where are you going?'" *John 16:5 KJV*

"And this is life eternal, that they might know You, the only true God, and Jesus Christ, whom You have *sent*." *John 17:3 KJV*

"As You have *sent* me into the world, even so have I also *sent* them into the world." *John 17:18 KJV*

"That they all may be one; as You, Father, are in me, and I in You, that they also may be one in us: that the world may believe that You have *sent* me." *John 17:21 KJV*

"I in them, and You in me, that they may be made perfect in one; and that the world may know that You have *sent* me, and have loved them, as You have loved me." *John 17:23 KJV*

"O righteous Father, the world has not known You: but I have known You, and these have known that You have *sent* me." *John 17:25 KJV*

Then said Jesus to them again, "Peace be unto you: as my Father has *sent* me, even so send I you." *John 20:21 KJV*

That God the Father *sent* God the Son is affirmed by both the Apostle Paul and the Apostle John:

{4} When the fullness of time had arrived, God *sent* His Son, made of a woman, made under the law, {5} to redeem those who were under the law, that we might receive the adoption of sons. *Galatians 4:4-5 KJV (Paraphrase)*

{9} In this was manifested the love of God toward us, because that God *sent* His only begotten Son into the world, that we might live through him. [10} Herein is love, not that we loved God, but that He loved us, and *sent* His Son to be the propitiation for our sins. {14} And we have seen and do testify that the Father sent the Son to be the Savior of the world. *1 John 4:9-10, 14 KJV*

3. The Prophesied Messiah

as Son of God

Jesus' birth as *the Messiah* was prophesied in Scripture. (The Holy Bible is the only true Scripture.)

Through many witnesses, the Holy Spirit established the lineage of the Christ (i.e., the Messiah or H'Moshiach) from Abraham through Isaac and Jacob to the tribe of Judah and out of the house of David *(Genesis 12:3, 18:18, 21:12, 22:18, 26:4, 28:14, 49:10; 2 Samuel 7:12-16; Psalms 18:50, 89:3-4, 89:20, 132:11; Isaiah 9:6-7, 11:1, 11:10; Jeremiah 23:5-6, 33:14-15).* Moreover, it was prophesied through Isaiah that the Messiah would be conceived by a virgin *(Isaiah 7:14).* It was prophesied through Micah that he would be born in Bethlehem *(Micah 5:2).* And it was prophesied through the typology in the third and sixth chapters of Zechariah that his name would be Yehoshuah [H3091] — from which is derived the Ionic Greek form "Iesous" [G2424], the Classical Latin form "Iesus" [IESVS], and the Early Modern English form "Jesus."

Many have testified of the Messiah's Sonship. It was prophesied by God's Holy Spirit through King David: "I will be his father, and he shall be My son" *(2 Samuel 7:14 KJV).* Through Isaiah: "Unto us a child is born, unto us a son is given" *(Isaiah 9:6 KJV).* Through the Angel Gabriel to Mary: "He shall be great, and shall be called the Son of the Highest" *(Luke 1:32 KJV)* and "The Holy Ghost shall come upon you [Mary]: therefore also that holy thing which shall be born of you shall be called 'the Son of God'" *(Luke 1:35 KJV).* John the Baptist bore record that Jesus was the Son of God *(John 1:32-34).* God the Father Himself testified twice of Jesus: "THIS IS MY BELOVED SON, IN WHOM I AM WELL PLEASED" *(Matthew 3:17, 17:5; Mark 1:11, 9:7; Luke 3:22, 9:35 KJV).* Saint Mark testified in his gospel: "Jesus Christ, the Son of God" *(Mark 1:1 KJV).* The bedrock of the Christian faith is found in the Apostle Peter's declaration to Jesus: "You are the Christ, the Son of the Living God" *(Matthew 16:16 KJV)*.

Even the unclean spirits recognized that Jesus Christ was the Son of God: "And, behold, they [the unclean spirits] cried out, saying, 'What have we to do with you, Jesus, you Son of God? Are you come here to torment us before the time [of the Final Judgment]?'" *(Matthew 8:29 KJV Paraphrase;* see also *Mark 3:11 & 5:7* and *Luke 4:41 & 8:28)*

To people who are living before *the Millennium:* Jesus Christ is the *only-begotten* Son of God. If you and I are ever faced with a choice between acknowledging that Jesus Christ is the *only-begotten* Son of God or our own beheading *(Revelation 20:4),* I pray that our Lord's power, force, and authority be within us and upon us so that we never refute this absolute, unequivocal, and eternal truth. Although our heads might be severed from our bodies, authentic Christian believers can never be severed from the Body of Christ if they remain true to the *only-begotten* Son of God.

Why is it so important for Satan to keep human beings from understanding that Jesus Christ is the *only-begotten* Son of God? Satan keeps them from accepting eternal salvation. Why does Satan rage against Christians? Satan rages because he is full of envy and because he hates the LORD God Almighty and seeks to rob Him of His creation. Although Satan can "ape," imitate, or mimic the one true and only real God in many ways, Satan is only an illusionist. Although Satan can spawn like-minded individuals through his cunning, evil, and hatred, he can never conceive a human being. Satan cannot create. Satan can only make monsters from the spiritually dead.

Moreover, Satan seeks to deny human beings eternal salvation because eternal salvation is something he himself cannot receive. Many people living before *the Millennium* do not understand that Satan is a liar, that Satan is the father of lying, and that Satan's native language is lying *(John 8:44).* Satan speaks lies by distorting the truth and disguising evil. In fact, Satan is the originator of deception, disinformation, misinformation, diversion, and fake news — all intended to reframe the good news of salvation through Jesus Christ so that unsaved people might be misled and, thereby, detoured away from receiving and accepting the gospel message of salvation through Jesus Christ.

Satan cannot bear the truth that Jesus Christ is the *only-begotten* Son of God.

4. The *Only-Begotten* Son of God

μονογενής (pronounced mo-no-ge-nase´) [G3439] is the most important word in the Greek New Testament when it is used in conjunction with the physical conception and birth of Christ Jesus as the Son of Yahweh, the God of the Holy Bible. μονογενής (mo-no-ge-nase´) is a compound word composed of the two base, or root, words μόνος (pronounced mo-nos´) [G3441] and γεννάω (pronounced gen-au´) [G1080]. μόνος (mo-nos´) means: *one, only, only one, one and only, solitary,* and *unique;* and γεννάω (gen-au´) means: *born* (i.e., delivered from a uterus), *begat, begotten, birthed, conceived, generated,* and *legitimate.*

Because μονογενής (mo-no-ge-nase´) is a compound word, its complete meaning includes the individual meanings of both root words and not just the meaning of one of them. In other words, the full definition for μονογενής (mo-no-ge-nase´) includes: *only-begotten, one and only physically born, only legitimate, uniquely-conceived,* and *solitarily-generated.* Although some Bible scholars have chosen to define μονογενής (mo-no-ge-nase´) by the single word *only* because they believe that the *begotten* portion is redundant, implied, archaic, and/or unrelatable to the modern ear, the definition *only* without *begotten* is, in fact, an undertranslation because it is missing one-half of its full meaning. To be sure, using the single word *only* to define μονογενής (mo-no-ge-nase´) does not impart the same meaning as using *only-begotten.*

Many people do not grasp the meaning of *begotten* in the expression *only-begotten Son of God.* Therefore, for the sake of clarity, it is important to state here that "begotten" is derived from Old English and is the past participle of the verb "beget," whose past tense is "begat" *(beget, begat, begotten).* The word *beget* means "to bear" *(bear, bore, born),* "to give birth to," and "to produce offspring."

Thus, the word "begotten" means "born," "birthed," "conceived," or "physically delivered from a uterus." The first man Adam was not "begotten" by the God of the Holy Bible because the first man Adam was neither conceived from a fertilized egg nor delivered from a uterus and because the first man Adam was neither self-existent nor equivalent to the Creator-God. Christ Jesus, however, is self-existent and equivalent to the Creator-God *(John 1:1 and 1:10)*. Only Christ Jesus was "the begotten" of God. Although the first man Adam was "the Son of God" *(Luke 3:38)*, the first man Adam was a created being and never God-in-flesh as was Christ Jesus *(John 1:14 KJV)*. (For the sake of clarity, *God-in-flesh* and *God-Incarnate* are synonymous.)

In the case of Christ Jesus, "begat by God" and "begotten by God" mean: (1) that God Himself provided the seed and Mary (Miriam) herself provided the egg for the conception of Christ Jesus; (2) that Christ Jesus was physically delivered from Mary's uterus; and (3) that Christ Jesus was composed of the same spiritual substance, nature, and essence as God the Father in addition to human flesh. Christ Jesus was not generated through sexual relations but through the Creator-God's Holy Spirit *overshadowing* Mary *(Luke 1:35 KJV)*. Mary the mother was a full participant in the conception and birth of Christ Jesus through her personal physical contributions of egg, uterus, and placental nutrition. Mary was not just an incubator into which a second created Adam had been placed. Although Yahweh is the Father and Mary is the mother of Christ Jesus, and Christ Jesus is God-in-flesh, Mary is neither *the wife of God* nor *the mother of God*. Christ Jesus was the unique hybrid of (1) the Creator-God's Holy Spirit and (2) Mary's corporeality (i.e., her physical body, substance, or form).

Although the first man Adam was *created* in the complete image and perfect likeness of the Creator-God, the first man Adam was not equal to the Creator-God. In other words, the first man Adam was not one with God. In contrast, Christ Jesus was composed of the same self-existent substance as God the Father and, as such, is uniquely one in *Being* with Him. Thus, Christ Jesus was, is, and always will be the same as God because he, in fact, is God Himself. The first man Adam was made only of *created* substance; in contrast, Christ Jesus was composed of the same self-existent substance as God, who uniquely appeared in flesh. (Christ Jesus was, is, and always will be God regardless of the state or condition of being that his personhood was, is, or will be in.)

In order to define *only-begotten* correctly concerning Christ Jesus, it is important to properly contextualize μονογενής (mo-no-ge-nase´) according to the writings of John the Apostle. Christ Jesus is known as "the Word of God" not only in Revelation 19:13 (written by John the Apostle) but also in the Gospel According to John:

{1} In the beginning was the Word, and the Word was with God, and the Word was God. {2} The same was in the beginning with God. {3} All things were made by him; and without him was not anything made that was made. {4} In him was life; and the life was the light of all people. {5} And the life's light had shone in darkness, but darkness could not comprehend it. {10} He was in the world, and the world was made by him, but the world did not recognize who he was. {14} And the Word was made flesh, and dwelt among us, and we beheld his glory — the glory as of the only begotten [μονογενής] of the Father, full of grace and truth. {18} No one has seen God at any time; the only begotten [μονογενής] Son, who is at the core of the Father, he has declared Him. {34} And I [John] saw him, and bare record that he is the Son of God. {49} And Nathanael responded to Jesus and said, "Rabbi [Teacher], you are the Son of God; you are the King of Israel." *John 1:1-5, 10, 14, 18, 34, & 49 KJV (Paraphrase)*

To summarize at this juncture:

1. Christ Jesus is "the *Word* of God" *(Revelation 19:13 KJV)*.

2. The *Word* of God is the Creator-God *(John 1:1 and 1:10 KJV)*.

3. *God the Son* is at the core ("in the bosom") of *God the Father (John 1:18 KJV)*.

4. The *Word* was made flesh as the only-begotten Son of God in Christ Jesus *(John 1:14, 18, 34, and 35 KJV)*.

5. Christ Jesus is God-Incarnate (i.e., God-in-flesh).

6. The Creator-God was in the world that he had made, but the world did not recognize him because those in darkness could not see his transfigured glory — the glory that John, James, and Peter had witnessed on the mountain when Christ Jesus spoke with Elijah and Moses *(John 1:4, 5, 10, and 14 KJV)*.

Because of his unique conception as the *only-begotten* Son of God, Christ Jesus is fully God and fully man. No one else can ever lay claim — or will ever be able to lay claim — to that singular status.

Some people concede that Christ Jesus *is* the Son of God but only to the same degree that other people in the Bible are referred to as Sons of God.

Three important examples follow:

Example One

(1) First, some people believe that Christ Jesus as the Son of God is no different from Adam because Adam is clearly referred to as "the Son of God" in Luke 3:38 (KJV).

However, in response to the argument that Adam was the Son of God, it is important to note that Adam was not *begotten* by God: Adam was created out of unformed matter, or *dust (Genesis 2:7 KJV)*. Adam was not born of a human mother. Christ Jesus is the only *begotten* Son of God. That means that Christ Jesus is the only Son of God who was begotten by God's Holy Spirit in consort with a human female. The God of the Holy Bible was the Father and Mary was the mother of Christ Jesus. Both God the Father and Mary the mother were equal physical contributors to the birth of Christ Jesus: Christ Jesus was begotten from a materialized seed (i.e., spermatozoon) provided by God the Father and from a physical egg (i.e., at an oocyte stage) provided by Mary the mother. Although the spermatozoon may have been materialized: (1) out of unformed matter (i.e., *de novo*), (2) out of chaos (i.e., *ex nihilo*), or (3) out of deific genetic manipulation, the egg was provided by Mary alone. Christ Jesus was not conceived by some strange form of spontaneous generation within Mary's womb. Christ Jesus was not conceived without Mary's haploid chromosomal contribution. Christ Jesus was not cloned from Mary.

Because many unsaved people's understanding of Christianity comes from their superficial exposure to Roman Catholicism, Eastern Orthodoxy, and Coptic (i.e., Egyptian) Christianity, they do not fully comprehend the concept of the three parts of the Godhead (i.e., God the Father, God the Son, and God the Holy Spirit). Because of the pagan idolatry of Mary that existed, and still exists, in Roman Catholicism, Eastern Orthodoxy, and Coptic Christianity, they erroneously conclude that Mary is considered by Christians to be the third part of the tri-unity of the God of the Holy Bible as "God the Mother" (in addition to God the Father and God the Son).

For the sake of clarification, regardless of the Mariolatry (i.e., pagan idolatry of Mary) that exists in Roman Catholicism, Eastern Orthodoxy, and Coptic Christianity, Mary is not considered to be "God the Mother" or the third part of the tri-unity of God anywhere in mainstream Christianity, not even in the three sects of Christianity just mentioned. All authentic Christians know that Mary was a human being, neither the wife of God nor the mother of God, and certainly was never part of the Godhead.

Example Two

(2) Second, some people believe that Christ Jesus as the *begotten* Son of God is no different from King David because they have erroneously concluded that King David was referred to as a *begotten* Son of God in Psalm 2:7:

> {6} Yet have I set My king upon My holy hill of Zion. {7} I will declare the decree: the LORD has said unto me, "You are My Son; this day have I begotten you. {8} Ask of Me, and I will give you the heathen for your inheritance, and the uttermost parts of the Earth for your possession. {9} You shall break them with a rod of iron; you will dash them into pieces like a potter's vessel."
> *Psalm 2:6-9 KJV (Paraphrase)*

People who think that Psalm 2 is referring to King David are mistaken. They don't understand that Psalm 2 is prophetic Scripture about the *King of kings* (i.e., the Messiah) and not about King David. In other words, the King referenced in Psalm 2:6 is Christ Jesus, and the "begotten Son" referenced in Psalm 2:7 is Christ Jesus, not King David. The LORD God Almighty clearly states in Psalm 2:8: "Ask Me, and I will give you the heathen for your inheritance, and the uttermost parts of the earth for your possession." The Hebrew word for "the heathen" (or "the nations" in other Bible translations) is "goyim" [H1471], which means "the Gentiles." King David did not rule over the Gentiles throughout the whole world (i.e., to "the uttermost parts of the Earth"): King David was the king over the children of Israel in the Holy Land. Only the Savior of the world, Christ Jesus, rules over Gentiles throughout the whole world. Psalm 2:9 confirms that the entire second psalm is about the Savior by referencing his rule of the whole world with "a rod of iron" *(Revelation 12:5; 19:15)*. To further confirm this understanding, whenever the *begotten* from Psalm 2:7 is referenced in the New Testament *(Acts 13:33, Hebrews 1:5,* and *Hebrews 5:5),* it is *always* concerning Christ Jesus and not King David.

For those who might question the use of μονογενής (pronounced mo-no-ge-nase´) and *begotten* in the Greek and English translations of the New Testament, it is important to add that the Septuagint version of the Old Testament (the Greek translation from the Hebrew) uses the Greek base, or root, word γεννάω (pronounced gen-au´) [G1080] in Psalm 2:7 to indicate that the prophesied Messiah would be "begotten."

Example Three

(3) Third, some unsaved people point to various verses in the Holy Bible to prove that there are other "Sons of God" besides Jesus Christ:

...the sons of God saw that the daughters of men were attractive, and they made wives of all that they chose. *Genesis 6:2 KJV (Paraphrase)*

They do not understand that the phrase "sons of God" here refers to angelic beings who left their first estate in Heaven to have sexual intercourse with human beings (see verse 6 of Jude). They also fail to understand that the phrase "sons of God" used in the New Testament *(John 1:12; Romans 8:14,19; Philippians 2:15; 1 John 3:1-2)* refers to people who are "heirs" of Christ Jesus (or "co-heirs" with him) through their faith in his atoning sacrifice.

In order to be saved, people can't just believe that Christ Jesus existed. People must believe that Christ Jesus is the *only-begotten* Son of God and accept him as their personal Savior. That is why the "blasphemies" written about in Revelation Chapter Thirteen are about blaspheming the God of the Holy Bible by telling Him that He cannot have an *only-begotten* Son. The Wrath of the God of the Holy Bible rests on those who tell Him that He cannot have an *only-begotten* Son and on those who tell Him that Christ Jesus is not His *only-begotten* Son.

{35} The Father loves the Son [Christ Jesus] and has given all things into his hand. {36} He who believes in the Son has eternal life; but he who does not obey the Son will not see life [in Heaven], but the wrath of God abides on him. [brackets mine] *John 3:35-36 KJV*

For as long as people on Earth consciously reject Christ Jesus as the *only-begotten* Son of Yahweh and God-Incarnate, they place themselves under the curse of Yahweh's Wrath (i.e., His Justified Anger) not only while they are on Earth but also throughout eternity. However, for the duration that souls are in corporeality (i.e., in a human body), they still have an opportunity (not necessarily just *one* opportunity) to remove themselves from the curse of Yahweh by: (1) accepting Christ Jesus as the *only-begotten* Son of Yahweh and God-Incarnate; and (2) accepting his sacrifice on the cross of Calvary as the only sacrifice acceptable to God the Father for the atonement of their iniquity and sins and the remission of the debt they owe for their iniquity and sins.

Satan and his demons do not mind if people accept that: (1) Christ Jesus is one prophet of many prophets; (2) Christ Jesus was born of a virgin (Mary); (3) Christ Jesus is the prophesied Messiah of Israel; (4) Christ Jesus was a worker of miracles; and (5) Christ Jesus will return one day to defeat the Antichrist, or False Messiah. However, Satan and his demons are adamant that no one on Earth learn that: (1) Christ Jesus is the *only-begotten* Son of God; (2) Christ Jesus is the only incarnation of God in flesh; (3) Christ Jesus is the Savior of the world; and (4) Christ Jesus is our personal Savior — all four concepts both explicitly and implicitly stated and restated in the New Testament.

By influencing human beings to reject the four concepts given in the previous paragraph, Satan helps confirm for Christians that, of all theological concepts, these four concepts are the most powerful for people on Earth to know. Why are they the most powerful? They threaten Satan in his mission to prevent the salvation of human beings and, thereby, rob Yahweh of the restoration of His fallen creation. To be sure, although Satan is the enemy of all human beings, Satan is only our indirect enemy; Satan's true Enemy is Yahweh, the God of the Holy Bible. It is for this reason that Satan seeks to rob Yahweh of His creation. Satan erroneously and foolishly believes that, by robbing Yahweh of His creation, Satan will unseat Yahweh as Supreme Being and replace Him as universal Sovereign.

Everything that Satan has done after his fall has been to fulfill his desire of robbing the Creator-God of His creation, unseat the Creator-God as Supreme Being, and replace the Creator-God as universal Sovereign. To this end, throughout history, Satan has tried to: (1) murder all Jews; (2) murder all Christians; (3) discredit the witness, or testimony, of Jews and Christians; (4) firmly establish secularism and false religion throughout the Earth; and (5) cause all people on Earth to doubt the accuracy of the Old and New Testaments and the validity of the gospel message of salvation through Christ Jesus alone as the *only-begotten* Son of God and God-in-flesh.

In transitioning to the next section, it is important for the reader to always remember that Christ Jesus is God-Incarnate. *That* is why Christ Jesus is worshiped. Christ Jesus said: "I am Alpha and Omega, the beginning and the end, and the First and the Last" *(Revelation 22:13 KJV)*. According to the unified language of the Holy Bible, saying "I am the First and Last" is equivalent to saying "I am God." *For example,* in Isaiah 41:4, the God of the Holy Bible states: "Who has wrought and done it, calling the generations from the beginning? I the LORD, the First, and the Last; I am He." And in Isaiah 44:6, God states: "Thus says the LORD the King of Israel, and his redeemer the LORD of hosts; I am the First, and I am the Last; and beside Me there is no God." Perhaps two of the most difficult concepts for non-Christians to understand about Christ Jesus include: (1) in Christ Jesus, the Creator-God inhabited a created body; and (2) the Creator-God resurrected the physical body of Christ Jesus after it was dead.

In closing this section, it is important to add that Christians are considered *begotten* children of God through their faith conversion in Christ Jesus as their personal Savior.

5. On the Supremacy of God

Throughout Old Testament history, God the Father rarely spoke directly to anyone. At times, He did speak directly to His prophets. However, when He did, He spoke to them: (1) through a cloud or fire covering provided by one or more of His holy angels; (2) via His Holy Spirit; and/or (3) by presenting Himself to His prophets in trancelike visions He induced in them. God the Father rarely spoke directly to human beings. He purposely hid Himself from us so our corporeality would not be expunged (i.e., annihilated) by His Holy and Fiery Presence.

During these New Testament times, God the Father primarily speaks to human beings through the recorded (i.e., written) gospel message of God the Son and to saved believers through His Holy Spirit *(saved believers* are people who have received/accepted Jesus Christ as their personal Savior). During these current times, God the Father still hides the Totality of His Being from souls in dust so that we are not expunged by His Holy and Fiery Presence.

Although God the Father's Glory was seen by three Apostles during the transfiguration of Jesus Christ on a mountain, God the Father's Heavenly Radiance was only partially seen there. The Totality, or Fullness, of God the Father's Fiery Being has never been seen by any human being, then or now. At the time of Jesus Christ's transfiguration, God the Father's voice also directly spoke to these three witnesses, saying: "This is My beloved Son: Hear him" Luke 9:35 KJV).

God the Son was given all power in Heaven and on Earth by God the Father. The only exception, or limit, to the jurisdiction of Jesus Christ was, and is, God the Father Himself. For this reason alone, God the Father has supremacy over God the Son, even though God the Son is at the very core of the one Supreme Being that we refer to as *Creator-God.* God the Father will only release His Holy and Fiery

Presence when Jesus Christ presents Heaven and Earth to Him at the end of his Millennial reign on Earth. Then, God the Father will become the *All* in the *all* that Jesus Christ has submitted to Him. God the Father will become *All-in-all* by infusing Himself throughout the entire universe. At that time, God the Father and God the Son will be indistinguishable from one another, much like they were before the beginning of the Genesis Creation.

Consistent with the supremacy of God the Father, most Bible-taught Christians pray for what they desire by praying to God the Father in the name of God the Son at the same time that they pray that His Will be done on Earth as it is already being done in Heaven. And they anticipate that their prayers will be answered through the agency of His Holy Spirit in accordance with His Will.

Regardless of anyone's desires to deny, ignore, or confuse the supremacy of God the Father over God the Son, Jesus Christ was quite clear that God the Father was, and is, greater than he (John 14:28) and that "no man knows the day and hour [when Jesus Christ will return], neither the angels in heaven nor the Son of God, but only God the Father" (Mark 13:32, see also Acts 1:7).

Confusing *God the Father's* role with *God the Son's* role comes with the failure of many Christians (i.e., most Oneness adherents and some Threeness adherents) to view the Father as one person and the Son as a separate person in the single, completely united Godhead. One cause for the confusion comes from believing that the English word *LORD* in the Old Testament is always synonymous with the English word *Lord* in the New Testament. Christians need to understand that the word *LORD* in the Old Testament and the word *Lord* in the New Testament are: (1) sometimes synonymous, (2) sometimes non-identical, and (3) sometimes equivocal (i.e., ambiguous).

In the Old Testament, the English word *LORD* is most often used in the King James Version to translate the Hebrew word יְהֹוָה YHWH [H3068] — which is a proper noun in Hebrew for the unpronounceable name of the Creator-God (specifically considered too holy to say aloud by Jews) — often transliterated as *Yahweh, Yehowah,* or *Yehovah.* YHWH can be translated as *the only Self-Existent One.*

Of the 6,519 times that the Hebrew word YHWH [H3068] is used in the Old Testament, it is translated 6,510 times in the King James Version as *LORD* (note the smaller uppercase used for the last three letters). When the Hebrew word YHWH [H3068] is encountered by Jews who are reading the Bible out loud, they often replace the word *Yahweh* with the Hebrew word *Adonai,* which means "Lord," "Respected One," "Sire," or "Sir."

When the English word *Lord* is used in the New Testament, it is translated from one of the twenty-two unique forms of the Greek word κύριος [G2962], which comes from the Greek word κύρος, meaning "supremacy," "having power," or "having authority." As such, the Greek word κύριος [G2962] means "anyone to whom service is due" or "anyone who has power and authority." The Greek word κύριος [G2962] is used as a title of respect with the following various meanings in the New Testament: (1) *LORD,* (2) *Lord,* (3) *lord,* (4) *Master,* (5) *master,* (6) *Owner,* (7) *owner,* (8) *Sire,* (9) *sire,* (10) *Sir,* and (11) *sir* (uppercase first letters here signifying *God the Father* [Yahweh] in some cases and *God the Son* [Christ Jesus] in other cases). The context of each specific passage in which the Greek word or its English translation is used determines its exact import. This helps to explain the ambiguity that exists for some, if not most, readers of the New Testament with regard to the Greek word κύριος [G2962] and the English word *Lord.* Again, sometimes the words κύριος and *Lord* are referring to the power and authority of God the Son and sometimes the words κύριος and *Lord* are referring to the power and authority of God the Father, who has conveyed His power and authority to God the Son for his absolute use in Heaven and on Earth (see Matthew 28:18 and 1 Corinthians 15:24):

Jesus came and spoke to them, saying: "All power is given unto me in Heaven and in Earth." Matthew 28:18 KJV

Then comes the end, when he [Jesus Christ] shall have delivered up the kingdom to God, even the Father; when he [Jesus Christ] shall have put down all rule and all authority and power. 1 Corinthians 15:24 KJV

Matthew 22:43-44 (KJV), Mark 12:36 (KJV), Luke 20:42-43 (KJV), and Acts 2:34-35 (KJV) quote King David from Psalm 110:1 (KJV) in their use of the Greek word κύριος for God the Father as well as for God the Son:

[King] David himself said by the Holy Ghost: "The LORD [κύριος here referring to God the Father] said to my Lord [κύριος here referring to God the Son]: 'Sit on my right hand [referring to an assigned position of power and authority] until I make your enemies your footstool.'"

In this book, entitled *The Threeness of God,* this written account of the supremacy of God the Father helps to explain the intellectual arguments that Oneness adherents have with many Threeness adherents and the arguments that some Threeness adherents have among themselves. (It should also be noted here that there are some non-Christian religions that take the concept of *Oneness* to a Satanic extreme in their false charge that Christianity is polytheistic when it recognizes the tri-unity of God.)

In closing, this written account of the supremacy of God the Father is not meant to take anything away from the omnipotence, omnipresence, or omniscience of God the Son — "in whom dwells all the fullness of the Godhead bodily" (Colossians 2:9). To be sure, the Word of God (Jesus Christ) is God Himself (John 1:1-5). To say that God the Father has all power and authority does not contradict that God the Son has all power and authority because, although God the

Father and God the Son are metaphysically partitioned from one another, they are also seamlessly united at the same time. Although this may be conceptually difficult to understand for beings who live on Earth, it is not difficult to understand for beings who already live in Heaven.

Finally, the present author closes this section on the supremacy of God with these oft-repeated words of Paul, Apostle to the Gentiles:

Grace be unto you, and peace, from God our Father, and from the Lord Jesus Christ. *Romans 1:7; 1 Corinthians 1:3; 2 Corinthians 1:2; Galatians 1:3; Ephesians 1:2; Philippians 1:2; Colossians 1:2; 1 Thessalonians 1:1; 2 Thessalonians 1:2; 1 Timothy 1:2; 2 Timothy 1:2; Titus 1:4;* and *Philemon 1:3 KJV*

To us there is but one God, the Father, of whom are all things, and we in Him; and one Lord Jesus Christ, by whom are all things, and we by him. *1 Corinthians 8:6 KJV*

God the Father sent God the Son and gave him supremacy in Heaven and on Earth (i.e., throughout all incorporeality and all corporeality).

6. Eternal Salvation

Central to Christianity is the doctrine of eternal salvation through the substitutionary blood atonement of Christ Jesus for the forgiveness of our sins and cancellation of the debt we owe to the God of the Holy Bible for our sins. Certainly, the Lamb of God's sacrifice does not relieve any one of us of our own burdens or responsibilities. Nor does it take away from the Apostle Paul's admonition for us to "work out our own salvation with fear and trembling" *(Philippians 2:12 KJV Paraphrase).*

What Christ Jesus did was reconcile us to God the Father that we might receive forgiveness — a restoration to fellowship with Him and all who belong to Him — through grace, God's unmerited favor. By resisting temptation all the way to Calvary, Christ Jesus was eternally victorious over the Tempter (i.e., the Devil or Satan). Through the self-sacrificing life that was in him, our Lord Jesus brought spiritual gifts for all who would believe on him. He paved the way for us back to our Creator. To say that Christ Jesus was just a mortal is far from the Truth. To say that Christ Jesus was not the *only-begotten* Son of God is a lie and blasphemy. To say that Christ Jesus did not die for our sins is heresy:

Who is a liar but the person who denies that Jesus is the Christ? He is antichrist that denies the Father and the Son. Whoever denies the Son, the same does not have the Father; but the person that acknowledges the Son has the Father also. *1 John 2:22-23 KJV*

Hereby know you the Spirit of God: every spirit that confesses that Jesus Christ is come in the flesh is of God: And every spirit that does not confess that Jesus Christ is come in the flesh is not of God: and this is that spirit of antichrist, whereof you have heard that it should come; and even now already is it in the world. *1 John 4:2-3 KJV*

The person who believes on the Son of God has the witness in himself/herself: the person who does not believe God has made God a liar because he/she does not believe the record that God gave of His Son. *1 John 5:10 KJV (Paraphrase)*

For many deceivers are entered into the world, who confess not that Jesus Christ is come in the flesh. This is the spirit of a deceiver and an antichrist. *2 John, verse 7 KJV*

7. The Name of God

Just because Jews and Christians may also call the Creator "God," "Theos," "Deus," "El," "Eloah," or "Elohim" does not mean that they do not know the Name of the God of the Holy Bible. The God of Jews and Christians identified Himself by name to Moses (Moshe) when Moses asked Him: "Who shall I say sent me?"

When asked for His name by Moses, God replied: "I AM THAT I AM," or EYEH ASHER EYEH [H1961] [H834] [H1961], and "Tell the children of Israel that "I AM," or EYEH [H1961], has sent you" *(Exodus 3:14)*. Regardless of how it is pronounced, the most holy Biblical name of God is YHWH [H3068] (often pronounced *Yahweh, Yehowah,* or *Yehovah); and* YHWH [H3068] is derived from EYEH [H1961]. The name YHWH is so holy to Jews that, instead of pronouncing it, they will either (1) substitute *Adonai* (i.e., "LORD") instead of reading it out loud or (2) substitute *H'Shem* (i.e., "the Name") when in conversation.

The *I AM* identity for the God of the Holy Bible is echoed by Christ Jesus when he answered the Jews who questioned his authority. Christ Jesus said: "Before Abraham was, I AM" *(John 8:58)*. Through his response, Christ Jesus clearly proclaimed himself to be one with the LORD God Almighty. Jesus did not say: "Before Abraham, I was" — which is to say: "I existed before Abraham" (although he clearly did). Rather, Christ Jesus was conveying that he exists in an eternal state of *being* in the Godhead and that "God the Son" is fully, completely, and perfectly one with "God the Father" yet not the same person (although the same *Being*.)

Jesus Christ, Christ Jesus, Jesus the Christ, and *Y'shua H'Moshiach* are all synonymous names for the only Messiah of Israel and one true Savior of the world.

To use the word *Jesus* alone when referring to the Savior is insufficient because there are ordinary mortals who possess the same name. Y'shua (Jeshua) [H3442] is derived from Yehoshuah (Jehoshua) [H3091] — of which: (1) "Iesous" [G2424] is the Ionic Greek form; (2) "Iesus" [IESVS] is the Classical Latin form; and (3) "Jesus" is the Early Modern English form. The Hebrew name Yehoshuah [H3091] means "YAH (or EYEH) is our salvation" — which is to say, "*the only Self-Existent One,* or the Great *I AM,* is our salvation."

To use the name *Christ* alone when referring to the Savior is insufficient because, when used alone, although it can accurately imply a spiritual state of mind and a heightened level of consciousness, it can also inaccurately imply that the spiritual state of mind and heightened level of consciousness may be achieved without accepting the Biblical Jesus as (1) the *only-begotten* Son of God, (2) the only Messiah of Israel, and (3) the one true Savior of the world. Indeed, one cannot have "the Christ," "the mind of Christ," "divine Mind," or "Christ Consciousness" without accepting the shed blood of the *only-begotten* Son of God as the only sacrifice acceptable to God the Father for the remission of our sins (i.e., the cancellation of the debt we owe to Him for our sins). To be sure, the crucifixion, or blood sacrifice, of Christ Jesus provides the only substitutionary offering acceptable to God the Father for our sins.

One cannot have "Jesus" without having "the Christ" and one cannot have "the Christ" without having "Jesus." Christians should always hold the whole name, "Jesus the Christ," while they simultaneously attend to its two parts: "Jesus" and "the Christ." The words *Jesus* and *Christ* are inextricably linked together and should rarely be used separately so as not to confuse the hearer, the reader, or even oneself (yes, we can easily confuse ourselves). The English word *Christ* is a title derived from the Greek word *Christos* [G5547] and its counterpart in Latin, *Christus* [CHRISTVS]. The Greek word *Christos* [G5547] is a translation of the Hebrew word *H'Moshiach* [H4899], which means "*the* Messiah" or "*the* Anointed One" in English. And the Greek word *Messias* [G3323] is the transliterated form of the Hebrew word *Moshiach* [H4899].

That both *God the Father* and *God the Son* have the same identity ("I AM") does not mean that they have the same personality or the same function in the universe even though they both have the same purpose and are co-equal parts of the triune Godhead along with *God the Holy Spirit.* Jesus the Christ said: "I and my Father are one" *(John 10:30 KJV).* To be sure, God the Father and God the Son are one, and they have the same identity ("I AM"), but they also have *Self*-assigned functions that are different from each other.

In the last sentence of the previous paragraph, I have capitalized the word *Self* to distinguish it as the sole identity of the Godhead, consisting of God the Father, God the Son, and God the Holy Spirit — the equivalent, consubstantial, and triadic elements of the one true and only real Supreme Being, Creator, and Lord of the Universe. (God the Father, God the Son, and God the Holy Spirit all possess the same *Being.*)

That "God the Father" and "God the Son" are one does not make them the same nor does it make them sequential manifestations of the Godhead to humanity. *God the Son* did not replace *God the Father.* And *God the Holy Spirit* did not replace *God the Son.*

Oneness Christians go to an extreme when they interpret "the LORD God is *one* LORD" *(Deuteronomy 6:4 KJV)* to mean that "God the Father" *is* "God the Son." Although Jesus Christ is: (a) the *only-begotten* Son of God *(John 3:16; Matthew 16:16);* (b) God-Incarnate *(Colossians 2:9; 1 Timothy 3:16);* and (c) one with God the Father *(John 17:11),* Jesus Christ *is not* God the Father. Although the two are one, they are not the same.

The theological position that *God the Son* replaced *God the Father* is untenable because it is unable to offer plausible explanations concerning: (1) the synchronous, or simultaneous, presence of *God the Father* and *God the Son* at the times when *God the Father* proclaimed: "This is My beloved Son in whom I am well pleased" *(Matthew 3:17; 17:5);* (2) to whom Jesus Christ was speaking from the cross when he said: "Father, forgive them for they do not know what they are doing"

(Luke 23:34 KJV); and (3) to whom Jesus Christ will deliver the Kingdom after *all* enemies of God have been finally conquered:

And when all things shall be subdued unto him *[God the Son]*, then shall the Son also himself be subject unto him *[God the Father]* that put all things under him *[God the Son]*, that God *[the Father]* may be all in all. [brackets mine] *1 Corinthians 15:28 KJV*

Jesus Christ is "the Word" and "the Word was, and is, God" *(John 1:1-5),* but Jesus Christ is not *God the Father.* The roles of *God the Father* and *God the Son* are different although the Father and the Son are one in the Godhead — along with the Holy Spirit — and all three serve the same Self-existent purpose.

To be sure, Christ Jesus ("God the Son") already has all authority and all power in Heaven and on Earth *(Matthew 28:27* and *Ephesians 1:22),* but not every enemy has been finally conquered yet, or "subdued unto him" *(1 Corinthians 15:28 KJV). For example,* the end-time Antichrist has not yet been overcome. And death, or mortality, itself remains to be conquered. Scripture teaches that the end-time Antichrist will be thrown into the Lake of Fire at the time of Christ Jesus' return to Earth *(Revelation 19:20).* Scripture also teaches that death, or mortality, is the final enemy that must and will be conquered *(1 Corinthians 15:26)* when, at the end of the coming Millennium of Peace, it — along with Hades (the current holding tank for unsaved souls) — will be thrown into the Lake of Fire at the time of the Great White Throne Judgment *(Revelation 20:11-14),* during which Judgment each remaining soul will either be assigned eternal salvation or eternal damnation.

The God of Jews and Christians has a specific name, found in God's response to Moses as well as in the specific name of *Jesus* for the Christ (i.e., the Messiah).

8. About Whom Shall We Testify?

Gone is the day when Christian people can refer to the God of the Holy Bible simply as *God* and others would know immediately about whom they were referring. To be sure, in this day and age, when authentic Christian people speak to one another about *God,* they know about whom they are speaking — but not everyone else knows. Nominal Christians do not know. Inauthentic Christians do not know. Secular Christians do not know. And, indeed, non-Christians do not know. Most people in this day and age do not know because: (1) they erroneously disbelieve that the God of the Holy Bible is the one true and only real God; (2) they erroneously believe that people from different world religions worship the same deity referred to as *God;* and/or (3) they automatically assume that, when anyone uses the word *God,* they are speaking about the God of the Holy Bible.

Christians must always remember that the *only-begotten* Son of God is "God-Incarnate," or "God-in-flesh" *(John 1:1-5, 14; 1 Timothy 3:16).*

If ever in doubt about which specific name of God to use, always use the expressions "Yahweh," "Jesus Christ," or "the Lord Jesus" in place of the generic word *God* and you will be sure not to inadvertently blaspheme the Holy Name of the one true and only real Creator-God, the God of the Holy Bible. It should also be reiterated here that, because some Messianic Jews (i.e., Christian Jews) may feel uncomfortable using the "unpronounceable" tetragrammaton (YHWH) when speaking, they might use Hebrew words like *Adonai* (i.e., "LORD") or *HaShem* (i.e., "the Name") for *God the Father* and *Y'shua H'Moshiach* (i.e., "Jesus the Messiah") for *God the Son.*

Authentic Christians do not belong to themselves. We do not own ourselves. We belong to Christ Jesus. It is Christ Jesus who owns us.

We were bought with a price, which price is the shed blood of God's *only-begotten* Son. Consequently, it is no longer we who live but Christ Jesus who lives within us *(Galatians 2:20b)* through God's indwelling Holy Spirit.

9. The Origin of God's Tri-Unity

The Supreme Being has always been One and will always continue to be One. However, before the beginning of creation — as recounted in Chapter One of Genesis — the Supreme Being partitioned Himself into: (1) *the LORD God*, (2) *the Spoken Word (the Logos),* and (3) *the Spirit.* Alternate titles for these three partitions include: *God the Father, God the Son,* and *God the Holy Spirit.* People who think that the Supreme Being's tri-unity is representative of three different deities are incorrect; they are using the wrong mathematical model for their conceptualization of tri-unity. Instead of $1 + 1 + 1 = 3$, the correct mathematical model for the tri-unity of God is $1 \times 1 \times 1 = 1^3$, or one raised to the third power (1^3). No member of this tri-unity operates independently of the other two. All three, in fact, are One.

The earliest identification in the Bible of the tri-unity of the Supreme Being is found in Genesis, Chapter One, verses 1 through 3:

{1} In the beginning God *[representing God the Father]* created the heaven and the earth. {2} And the earth became formless and void; and darkness was upon the face of the deep. And the Spirit of God *[representing God the Holy Spirit]* moved upon the face of the waters. {3} And God *said [representing God's Spoken Word, the Logos, God the Son,* or *the pre-incarnate Christ]:* "Let there be light: and there was light." [brackets and italics mine]

That *the Spoken Word* in Genesis 1:3 is *the Son of God* is confirmed in the Gospel According to John, Chapter One, verses 1 and 14:

{1} In the beginning was the Word *[the Logos* or *pre-incarnate Christ]*, and the Word *[the Logos* or *pre-incarnate Christ]*, was with God, and the Word *[the Logos* or *pre-incarnate Christ]*, was

God. {14} And the Word *[the Logos* or *pre-incarnate Christ],* was made flesh, and dwelt among us — and we beheld his glory [at the time of his transfiguration on the mountain], the glory of the only-begotten of the Father, full of grace and truth. [brackets mine]

In confirmation, Christ Jesus is also called *the Word of God* in Revelation 19:13:

And he [Christ Jesus] was clothed with a vesture dipped in blood: and his name is called *the Word of God [the Logos of God].* [brackets and italics mine]

The Creator-God partitioned Himself before the beginning of His creation in order to effect His Plan of Salvation for Adamic souls whom He foreknew would fall from immortality to mortality. In establishing His Plan of Salvation, the Creator-God wanted to retrieve all fallen eternal souls who would eventually repent of their waywardness in exalting themselves and, instead, return to exalting Him.

At the time of the end (after the millennial reign of Christ Jesus on Earth), when all that is to be restored to the Creator-Savior has been restored, *God the Father* will then infuse the Totality of His Fiery Being (i.e., *His Holy and Fiery Presence*) into the "all" that He placed under the feet of *God the Son.* At that time, there will no longer be partitions of the Supreme Being or separation of the Supreme Being from His created souls because the Creator-God will then be *All-in-all.* Although the Creator-God is "All," He is not technically "in all" until the time that Christ Jesus' millennial rule on Earth is over. This infusion and reunification is attested to in 1 Corinthians, Chapter Fifteen, verses 24 through 28:

{24} Then comes the end, when he *[God the Son]* shall have delivered up the kingdom to God, even the Father — when he

[God the Son] shall have put down all rule and all authority and power. {25} For he *[God the Son]* must reign until He *[God the Father]* has put all enemies under his *[God the Son's]* feet. {26} The last enemy that shall be destroyed is death. {27} For He *[God the Father]* has put all things under his *[God the Son's]* feet. But when he says all things are put under him *[God the Son]*, it is manifest that He *[God the Father]* is excepted who put all things under him *[God the Son]*. {28} And when all things shall be subdued unto him *[God the Son]*, then shall the Son also himself be subject unto Him *[God the Father]* who put all things under him *[God the Son]*, that God may be All in all. [brackets mine]

To be sure, Christ Jesus *(God the Son)* already has all authority and all power in Heaven and on Earth *(Matthew 28:27; Ephesians 1:22)*, but not every enemy has been finally conquered yet, or "subdued unto him" *(1 Corinthians 15:28 KJV)*. *For example:* (1) the end-time Antichrist has not yet been overcome. (That will not happen until the beginning of *the Millennium,* when Christ Jesus returns*)*. And (2) *death* — not just physical death but the entire state of mortality itself — remains to be expunged. (That will not happen until the end of *the Millennium.)*

Scripture teaches that the Antichrist will not be thrown into the Lake of Fire until the time of Christ Jesus' return to Earth *(Revelation 19:20)*. Scripture also teaches that *death,* or the state of mortality, will not be conquered until the end of the millennium of peace, when *death* — along with Hades (the current holding tank for unsaved fallen souls) — will be thrown into the Lake of Fire at the time of the Great White Throne Judgment *(1 Corinthians 15:26; Revelation 20:11-14)*, during which time each remaining soul will either be assigned to a state of eternal redemption or a state of eternal damnation.

At this juncture, it is important to note that the Creator-God, His created beings (including His re-created, or saved, beings) are fully united only when the Creator-God becomes *All-in-all.* This does not mean that the Creator and His created become the same Being even though they are both spiritual in nature. All it means is that the substance of created beings is distinguishably miscible in the substance of the Creator. (The meaning and relevance of the word *miscible* is explained in Section 10.)

In summary: The complete re-union, or unpartitioning, of the three persons of God will not take place until the end of *the Millennium.* The complete union of the Creator and His created also does not take place until the end of *the Millennium,* when God the Father unleashes the full power of His Fiery Being into the physically-observable universe.

Author's Notes

The partitioning of the Creator-God took place in the absolute space-time of eternity whereas the Genesis creation (i.e., the beginning of the physically-observable universe) took place in the relative space-time of temporality. Once something takes place in eternity, it is as if that something has always existed there. Although sequences of related events occur in relative space-time, such timed sequences do not occur in states of being in the absolute space-time of eternity: States of *being* in eternity are different from states of *existence* in temporality.

Therefore, because the partitioning of the Creator-God into Father, Son, and Holy Spirit took place in eternity, we cannot determine exactly when the partitioning took place in relation to the Genesis creation. Because Father, Son, and Holy Spirit are present at the beginning of the Genesis creation (as indicated by Genesis 1:1-3): (1) either the Creator-God's partitioning took place before the beginning of the Genesis creation or (2) at the very instant the beginning of the Genesis creation took place (i.e., synchronously with the events in Genesis 1:1-3).

However, Christ Jesus spoke of his existence "before the foundation of the world" *(John 17:24 KJV)* — translated from the Greek πρὸ καταβολῆς κόσμου *(pro katabolis kosmou)* [G4253] [G2602] [G2889] — which can also be translated as "before the beginning of the physically-observable universe (i.e., cosmos)." The Apostle Paul used the same Greek phraseology in Ephesians 1:4 when speaking about the souls whom God the Father chose in Christ Jesus "before the beginning of the universe." And the Apostle Peter used the same phraseology in 1 Peter 1:20 when he stated that, although Christ Jesus was "foreordained before the beginning of the universe," he was manifested in these last times in order that we might be redeemed by his blood (read 1 Peter 1:18-21 KJV).

The three verses cited in the previous paragraph support that the partitioning of the Creator-God occurred not at the beginning of the physically-observable universe but *before* its creation.

In sum at this juncture:

(1) The partitioning of the Creator-God took place before the creation of the physically-observable universe.

(2) The Creator-God's Plan of Salvation was devised before the creation of the physically-observable universe.

(3) Before the creation of the physically-observable universe, the Creator-God foreknew that Adamic souls would fall from immortality to mortality.

The Tri-Unity of God

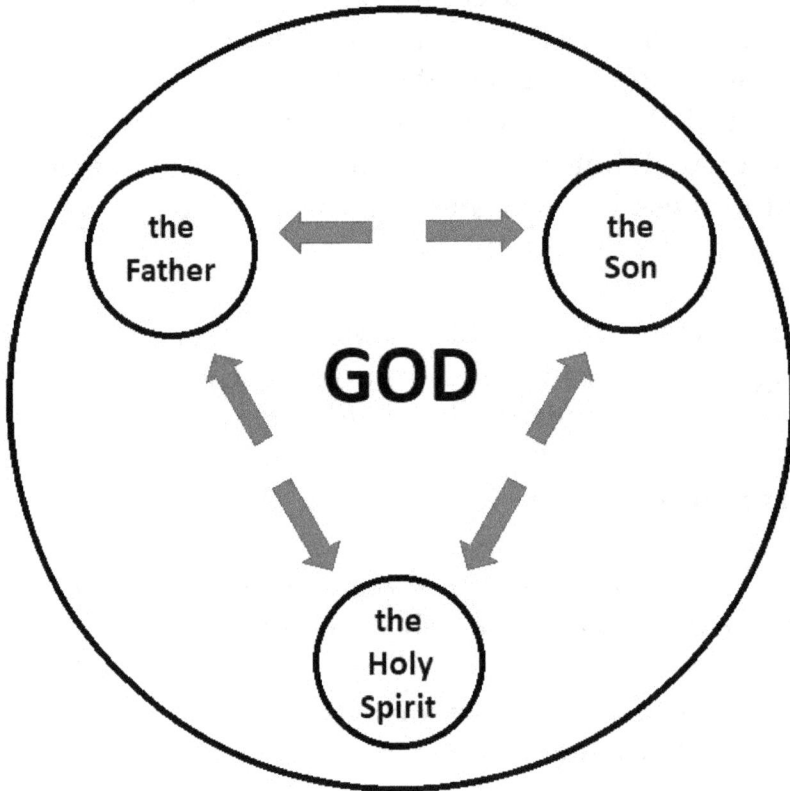

⬅➡ represents "is one with"

From "The Threeness of God"

©2021 by Rev. Joseph Adam Pearson, Ph.D.

www.christevangelicalbibleinstitute.com/English3.pdf

10. The Godhead's Forgiveness and Empathy

The Logos manifesting as God the Son achieved two things: (1) by providing the only unblemished sacrifice acceptable to God the Father for the forgiveness of sins; and (2) by conveying to the entire Godhead what it feels like to be tempted while in flesh.

(1)

Without a synchronously tripartite Godhead, there could be no salvation. Without God the Father accepting the crucifixion of God the Son as payment for the forgiveness of sins, there would be no redemption. In order to have a gift given, there must be a willing gift-giver and a willing gift-recipient. In order to have an acceptable sacrifice, there must be an acceptable sacrifice as well as an authority who confirms the acceptability of that sacrifice. The sacrifice of the unblemished only-begotten Son was the only sacrifice that could be assessed as acceptable by God the Father for the forgiveness of the sins of humankind.

The Godhead foreknew that the Adamic Race would turn from Him by going against His Will. He also knew that He would require an acceptable offering to propitiate His Wrath (i.e., appease His Justifiable Anger) against them if they were ever to be returned to Him. For these reasons, the Godhead devised a Plan that included the shedding of innocent blood to atone for and remit (i.e., "cover" and "cancel completely") all debts for their transgressions against Him. In order to execute His Plan of Salvation, the Godhead partitioned Himself before the creation into YHWH (to be known later as "LORD" and "the Father"), the Logos (to be known later as "the Word," "Lord," and "the Son of God"), and the Spirit (to be known later as "the Holy Ghost" and "the Holy Spirit").

When Christ Jesus bore the transgressions of human beings upon the cross of his crucifixion, that was the only instant in eternity that God the Father had to turn away from the Logos portion of the Godhead and the only instant in eternity that the Logos would be unaware of God the Father's Holy and Fiery Presence. If the Holy and Fiery Presence of God the Father were to look upon sin in our relative space-time, the bearer of that sin would be forever annihilated. The instant that Christ Jesus bore all of mankind's transgressions (past, present, and future) upon the cross, it was the only moment in eternity that he was unaware of God the Father's Holy and Fiery Presence, which — until that moment — burned effortlessly within his soul because of his sinlessness. It was this brief separation, when God the Father turned away from God the Son, that caused the Logos to cry out upon the cross: "Eli, Eli, lama sabachthani! My God, My God, why have you forsaken me?" *(Matthew 27:46 KJV; see also Psalm 22:1)*

Regardless of God the Father's "looking away" from the Logos for that one brief instant, and regardless of the Logos being unaware of God the Father's Holy and Fiery Presence for that moment, both YHWH and the Logos ("the Father" and "the Son") remained connected by the Holy Spirit. Because God the Son was doing the Will of God the Father in paying the penalty for transgressions against the Godhead, God the Holy Spirit still rested upon him even though His Holy and Fiery Presence had to be hidden from him. Although this was somewhat similar to the way in which God the Father covered Moses to protect him *(Exodus 33:21-23)*, the Holy and Fiery Presence of God the Father was totally eclipsed from God the Son as he bore our sins upon the cross, which is why Christ Jesus felt so utterly and completely forsaken.

Since it was not the role of the Holy Spirit to bear the iniquity and sin of humankind but was the role of God the Son to do so, and since the Holy Spirit still rested upon God the Son because he was doing God the Father's Will, God the Father remained connected — as God the Father forever remains connected — to God the Son by way of His Holy Spirit. And God the Son remained connected — as God the Son forever remains connected — to God the Father by way of His Holy

Spirit.

The penalty for all human transgressions against the Creator-God had to take place in flesh because the transgressions of Adam and Eve took place in their created flesh (which, of course, had a very different appearance in its original state than it does now). This explains the need for the Creator-God's Logos to be born in flesh as a human being in order to carry the full weight of the penalty for the transgressions of immortal beings who had become mortal beings as a result of their transgressions.

Transgressions against the Creator-God must always be paid for in the modality, or condition, in which they are committed. *For example:* (1) Because Lucifer and the angels who rebelled against the Creator-God did so in a spiritual state of being, and they remained in that spiritual state of being, their penalty must be exacted in that modality. (2) Because Adamic souls who rebelled against the Creator-God resulted in their current physical condition, their penalty necessitates payment in that modality (which is to say, in physicality or corporeality). At this point, it is important to reiterate that the original flesh of the Adamic Race and their original state of being were vastly different from what we know and experience today (see the subsection entitled *Astral Gelatinous™* in Section 11 of this book).

If human beings blaspheme against God's Holy Spirit, the sin is unforgivable *(Matthew 12:31-32)* because it is committed in our spirit (just like the transgressions of Lucifer and his angels are unforgivable because they were committed in their spirit). For the sake of clarification, "blasphemy against the Holy Spirit" is ridiculing the Creator-God's Holy Spirit by calling His Holy Spirit a liar and saying that His Holy Spirit is reprehensible and evil, when the reality is that His Holy Spirit is the only teacher of all truth *(John 16:13; 1 John 2:27)* and provides the only way that human beings can know the Creator-God and His Will as well as comprehend His Compassion and His Goodness while they are on Earth.

Careful (which is to say, deliberate), conscious, and continued rejection of the Creator-God's Plan of Salvation by renouncing God the Son and the Creator-God's Plan of Salvation all the way to one's deathbed falls within the category of "blasphemy against the Creator-God's Holy Spirit" (i.e., rejecting the call of the Holy Spirit to accept the role of Christ Jesus for one's salvation). Ignorance, or lack of awareness of the Creator-God's Plan of Salvation, because one has never heard it explained, or taking one's own life in the darkness of emotional despair, mental depression, and/or extreme physical pain does NOT constitute "blasphemy against the Creator-God's Holy Spirit." Although the shed blood of God the Son covers all of the sins of the world (that is, sinning in the body), it does not cover spiritual sin (that is, sinning in the spirit). That is why blasphemy against the Creator-God's Holy Spirit is unforgiveable.

(2)

Like His creation, the Creator-God evolves and will continue to evolve, and we will continue to evolve with Him. Before the Logos came to Earth as God the Son, the Godhead had never experienced temptation before. Because the Creator-God is omniscient, He knew what temptation was, and is, and could have dictated a highly accurate 100,000 volume encyclopedia about it. But the Creator-God's knowledge of temptation was only academic — which is to say, it was not experiential (i.e., personal and intimate by having been tempted Himself). However, through the experiences of Christ Jesus, the Creator-God's knowledge of temptation is now not only academic but also experiential as well: What God the Son learned about temptation while he was in corporeality was shared synchronously and simultaneously throughout the Godhead.

The Creator-God evolves Himself. He evolves His creation. He evolves His created beings. He even evolves our human understanding of Him. The Creator-God is neither too big for human beings to understand nor too small for them to overlook. He is just the right size. By permitting us to experience and overcome evil for ourselves, He brought us closer to His divine level of knowledge and understanding. Although we can never become the Creator-God, we can become more like Him and, thereby, make a more suitable eternal companion for Him — individually, collectively, and corporately.

By permitting Himself to experience temptation through the human experiences of God the Son, God the Father also brought Himself closer to us in His empathy for us. Through the life experiences of Jesus Christ, the entire Godhead now knows experientially what it means to be vulnerable to temptation while in human flesh. As God-in-flesh, Christ Jesus himself was touched with and by our infirmities *(Matthew 8:17; Hebrews 4:15)*. To be sure, the Creator-God's eternal mercy flows to us first and foremost through the shed blood of His only-begotten Son, but it is also effluent because of His firsthand understanding of our condition in corporeality — learned through the earthly experiences of His only-begotten Son. The entire Godhead experienced temptation, victimization, and the shedding of innocent blood personally through God the Son.

That the Creator-God evolves and will continue to evolve is not in conflict with the truth that God never changes. To be sure, the Creator-God's substance, nature, and essence never change, but He continues to consciously expand and evolve the substance, nature, and essence of His Supreme Being. The Creator-God is ever-expansive experientially. If you think about it, this is what we should expect from a Godhead that is dynamic and not static. His divine Mind remains insatiably inquisitive and curious at the same time that it is creative. The Creator-God continues to create and expand Himself into His ever-expanding spiritual universe. The totality of an ever-evolving and ever-expanding Creator-God can only fit into the totality of an ever-evolving and ever-expanding Creation.

For readers who may feel offended for the Creator-God because the present author has stated that His divine Mind is "insatiably inquisitive and curious," and who feel that this statement is inconsistent with His omniscience, please know that the Creator-God endowed created beings with free will so that He might interact *with* them as well as be challenged *by* them. The Creator-God was not going to be content with just observing His created beings; He wanted, and continues to want, to interact with them. To be sure, the Creator-God wants an eternal companion in us all individually, collectively, and corporately, but He does not want His eternal companion to be predictable, mechanical, and robotic. It pleases the Creator-God to interact with the free-will and creativity with which He has endowed us, especially when they are used to honor Him by reflecting and magnifying Him. Indeed, the Creator-God is the original and ongoing source of all of our individual, collective, and corporate free-will and creativity.

The Creator-God evolves but does not devolve. Unlike the fallen members of His original creation, the Creator-God cannot devolve. Devolution can only occur in segments, aspects, and parts of His creation when created beings consciously choose to depart from the Creator-God by stepping outside of His Will through disobedience. Of course, devolution happened to Lucifer and the angels who fell with him as well as to the Adamic Race; and devolution continues to happen to the spirits of human beings who consciously (i.e., willfully) reject the Creator-God by rejecting His Plan of Salvation and, thereby, disobey His Supreme and Sovereign Will. As a result of their irrevocable rejection of God the Son, the souls of all eternally-reprobate human beings become the *demons, devils,* and *unclean spirits* described in the Holy Bible (all three terms are used synonymously within this book as well as throughout the Holy Bible).

Once we know the Creator-God through the shed blood of Christ Jesus, we can never *unknow* Him although we can stop experiencing His goodness and mercy. Through the shed blood of Christ Jesus, the Creator-God becomes and remains our universal Self, Selfhood, Essence, and Being. As free-will beings created by the Creator-God, we can choose to evolve and expand along with Him and become what He would have us become, or we can resolutely choose to disobey Him — in which case, we still know who the Creator-God is but not by being a part of Him. Then, the Creator-God's Glory, or Holy and Fiery Presence, becomes a terror to us and our separation from Him becomes an eternal nightmare filled only with the spiritual horror that permanently eludes light, forgiveness, hope, joy, and love.

11. The Nature of God in Relation to His Post-Millennial Creation

Although the nature, substance, or essence of the Godhead (i.e., Spirit) transcends the nature, substance, or essence of physical existence (i.e., matter and physical energy), it is permissible to use physical characteristics and properties in figurative language to metaphysically illustrate (1) God's spiritual substance and (2) His relationship with His creation. In other words, characteristics and properties of physical nature can be used in analogies and metaphors to describe and illustrate characteristics and properties of God's spiritual nature, substance, or essence as well as the spiritual nature, substance, or essence of His created beings. The permissibility of metaphysical analogies and metaphors using physical nature is confirmed by the following Scripture:

> The invisible things of God from the creation of the world are clearly seen, being understood by the things that are made [i.e., physically created], *even* His eternal power and Godhead. *Romans 1:20 KJV*

The Partitioned versus Non-partitioned Godhead

The word *consubstantial* — meaning "having the same nature and essence and, therefore, made of the same substance" — has been translated from ὁμοούσιον *(homoousion)*, the accusative case form of the Greek word ὁμοούσιος *(homoousios)*. The word *co-essential* is also translated from the Greek word ὁμοούσιος *(homoousios)* and has two different senses, imports, or significations: (1) "of equal importance" *(meaning a)* as well as (2) "having the same nature and essence and, therefore, made of the same substance" *(meaning b)*. In relation to the Godhead, *nature, substance,* and *essence* denote Spirit (i.e., the

59

nature, substance, or essence of the Supreme Being) and are used synonymously; they describe *spiritual/invisible nature, spiritual/ invisible substance,* and *spiritual/invisible essence* — in contrast to words that describe *physicality, materiality, corporeality, matter,* and *physical energy.*

From the beginning of the physical creation until the end of *the Millennium:* (1) *God the Father* and *God the Son* are co-equal parts of the triune Godhead along with *God the Holy Spirit (co-essential: meaning a).* (2) All three parts of the Godhead are equal in importance *(co-essential: meaning a).* And (3) all three parts of the Godhead have the same nature, substance, or essence *(co-essential: meaning b and consubstantial).* As a reminder, the Godhead partitioned Himself into three parts, or *persons,* before manifesting His creation in order to effect a Plan of Salvation for created beings whom He foreknew would fall during the Adamic Fall but not for created beings who fell during the Luciferian Fall. [As a side note here, in describing the Godhead before the time He partitioned Himself, the descriptor *Oneness* can be used without raising objections or presenting contradictions.]

Although they were, and are, co-essential and consubstantial, God the Son held a subordinate role to God the Father when he was on Earth. It was this subordinate role on Earth that caused Christ Jesus to state: "My Father is greater than I" *(John 14:28b KJV)* and "But of the day and hour of Christ's return knows no man: no, neither the angels which are in heaven nor the Son, but only the Father" *(Mark 13:32 KJV Paraphrase; see also Acts 1:7).* To be sure, God the Son remains in this subordinate role even though all authority "in heaven and in earth" has been placed under his feet by God the Father *(Matthew 28:18 KJV).* God the Son remains in this subordinate role until the *Totality of the Father's Fiery Being* (i.e., *His Holy and Fiery Presence*) infills the entire creation placed by the Father under the Son's feet *(Matthew 28:18)* — which fulfills 1 Corinthians 15:28 at the end of *the Millennium:*

And when all things shall be subdued unto him *[God the Son],* then shall the Son also himself be subject unto Him *[God the*

Father] who put all things under him *[God the Son],* that God may be All in all. [brackets mine] *1 Corinthians 15:28 KJV*

In sum at this juncture: The Hebrew-Christian Deity, who is the God of the Holy Bible, and who is partitioned into Father, Son, and Holy Spirit, has distributed authority, jurisdiction, and responsibility differently within his three component parts. God the Father has mutually agreed-upon authority, jurisdiction, and responsibility over certain things; God the Son has mutually agreed-upon authority, jurisdiction, and responsibility over certain things; and God the Holy Spirit has mutually agreed-upon authority, jurisdiction, and responsibility over certain things. They are all One and in One, but the Godhead (consisting of Father, Son, and Holy Spirit) chose to distribute authority, jurisdiction, and responsibility differently into the three component parts. This explains why, in response to his Apostles questioning when Israel would be restored, Christ Jesus replied: "It is not for you to know the times or the seasons, which the Father has put in His own power" *(Acts 1:7 KJV Paraphrase).* This also explains why Christ Jesus said: "My Father is greater than I" *(John 14:28 KJV),* and why the Father exempted Himself when He placed all things under the feet (sovereignty) of Christ Jesus *(1 Corinthians 15:27).*

All three parts of the Godhead are composed of the same spiritual substance: they have the same invisible essence or nature. After 1 Corinthians 15:28 has been fulfilled, the three parts of the Godhead will no longer be identifiable, distinguishable, or partitioned from one another. That is why the Book of Revelation equivocally (i.e., ambiguously) states that the light in the spiritual city of New Jerusalem is the same glory, or spiritual light, from *God the Father* as that from *God the Son:*

And the city had no need of the sun, neither of the moon, to shine in it: for the glory of God did lighten it, and the Lamb is the light thereof. *Revelation 21:23 KJV*

All three partitioned parts of the Godhead are composed of the same spiritual substance with the same nature and essence: the spiritual molecules that make up the entire Godhead are indistinguishable and unidentifiable from one another even though the molecules are currently partitioned into *God the Father, God the Son,* and *God the Holy Spirit.* The spiritual molecules that make up the entire Godhead are: (1) all exactly the same (i.e., identical), (2) have the same spiritual polarity and spiritual intermolecular attractions and interactions, and (3) are spiritually *miscible* with one another (see the next paragraph for an explanation of *miscible).* [As a side note here, based on these three suppositions, the descriptor *Oneness* can be used in describing the Godhead without raising objections or presenting contradictions.]

In the previous paragraph, *miscible* is a term borrowed from the chemistry division of natural science that refers to fluids that do not separate into component parts or phases when they are combined. *For example:* (1) two glasses of water can be combined without their separation from one another because they are composed of identical molecules; the water molecules are *miscible* with one another because they are all identical. And (2) one glass of water and one glass of ethanol (i.e., drinking alcohol) can be combined without separation from one another even though they are composed of non-identical molecules; water and ethanol are *miscible* in one another because they each consist of molecules small enough to slide over one another without constraints from gravity or intermolecular forces. In other words, the water and ethanol molecules remain in solution with one another *ad infinitum* without separating out into two different component parts or phases (provided, of course, they are in a sealed container and not heated to boiling or cooled to freezing).

In sum at this juncture: Similar to the mixing of two glasses of water with one another, the substance of the three parts of the Godhead are indistinguishably miscible in each other (i.e., one cannot tell a difference in their individual nature, substance, or essence). Thus, after the fulfillment of 1 Corinthians 15:28 at the end of *the Millennium,* the three parts of the Godhead will no longer be partitioned from one another. [As a side note here, in describing the Godhead on the basis of its nature, substance, or essence, the descriptor *Oneness* can be used without raising objections or presenting contradictions.]

Theions

"Divine substance" is Spirit (i.e., the Creator-God's Holy Spirit) and "divine energy" is the *eternal energy, divine fire,* or *glory* of the Godhead. In the Greek New Testament: (1) *Theos* (θεός) means "the supreme Divinity;" (2) *Theios/Theiotes* (θεῖος/θειότης) means "Godhead;" and (3) *Theion* (θεῖον) means "divine fire," which is "the *eternal energy* or *glory* of the Creator-God."

In this book, the anglicized word *theion* (the English plural form is *theions*) provides a useful neologism. A *neologism* is "a newly-devised word or a new sense to an already existing word." For the purpose of *The Threeness of God,* a *theion* is "the smallest indivisible unit of divine, or eternal, energy." (This definition satisfies the "new sense" aspect of a *neologism.*) The following metaphysical analogy (or parallelism) might be helpful to the reader or listener: "a *theion* is to divine energy and divine light as a *photon* is to physical energy and physical light." In other words, just as a *photon* is a force-carrying, massless particle in the physically-observable universe, so is a *theion* a force-carrying, massless particle in the spiritually-observable universe (i.e., Spirit).

One measure of the utility of the *photon* to *theion* comparison arises in the capacity of the units to self-propagate or not. Because photons are not able to self-propagate and *theions* are able to self-propagate, the *photon* to *theion* comparison is less than perfect. However, the comparison is still useful, and conceptualizing *theions* provides a practical paradigm for understanding one aspect of divine substance and divine energy in Spirit.

63

For the sake of clarification, the reason that *theions* are able to self-propagate is that they are composed of divine love in addition to divine light. (Indeed, divine light and divine love are inseparable and are only mentioned here separately for the sake of discussion.) The Creator-God Himself is composed of *theions*. Thus, the Creator-God's very nature, substance, or essence includes His innate desire to self-propagate — or, in this case, to make created beings in His complete image and perfect likeness (as a reflection, or mirror-image, of Him). To be sure, this desire is borne of His divine love. His divine love wants (no, *needs*) to be shared with others in fellowship, communication, compassion, tenderness, mercy, grace, and care (but not as an enabler). Because the Creator-God *is* divine Love *(1 John 4:8 and 4:16)*, He wants (no, *needs*) to share the largess of it with beings created in His complete image and perfect likeness (as a reflection, or mirror-image, of Him).

The only danger in understanding this paradigm of *theions* is in the self-deluded conclusion that one can know the unknowable or can reduce the omnipotent, omniscient, and omnipresent Creator-God to one's own terms of understanding. What guards against operating in this misguided conclusion is one's ability to live in a state of perpetual contrition, which state is contrary to the fallen nature of being human but very much a part of the unfallen nature of being divine — that is, *not* being the Creator-God but being a part of the spiritual creation of the Creator-God — which includes being recast in the complete image and perfect likeness of the Creator-God (as His reflection, or mirror-image) through the shed blood of Christ Jesus.

Theoretically, if matter and physical energy could exist in Spirit, they would be instantly annihilated and disappear as if they had never existed. Just as "flesh and blood cannot inherit the Kingdom of God" *(1 Corinthians 15:50 KJV)* so also matter and physical energy cannot exist in Spirit. In a way, the Creator-God's *theions* act metaphysically as a kind of antimatter to matter. That is why no human being can look at God's face (i.e., His fiery appearance) and live *(Exodus 33:20 and Isaiah 6:5 KJV)*.

The Reflection, or Mirror-Image, of God

The nature, substance, or essence of God's spiritual creation is similar but not identical to the nature, substance, or essence of the Godhead. Figuratively and metaphysically, it is as if the spiritual molecules of the Godhead are all clockwise (i.e., right-handed or dextrorotary) and the spiritual molecules of His spiritual creation are all counter-clockwise (i.e., left-handed or levorotary). This especially makes sense since God's spiritual creation is a reflection, or mirror image, of Him. Figuratively and metaphysically, it is as if the entire Godhead is dextrorotary and His entire spiritual creation is levorotary (see the following paragraph for definitions of *dextrorotary* and *levorotary*). Although the two kinds of spiritual molecules are miscible in one another, they are eternally distinguishable from one another: Thus, although created beings cannot ever become the Creator-God (neither individually nor collectively), they can be joined to Him.

In the previous paragraph, *dextrorotary* and *levorotary* are terms borrowed from the chemistry division of natural science. They refer to molecules identical in atomic composition and molecular formulas (i.e., as isomers) but not identical spatially because they are geometric mirror images of one another — just like our right and left hands are identical structurally but not spatially. Thus, the spiritual substance of God's created beings is eternally distinguishable from the spiritual substance of the Godhead even though they are miscible in one another. Like the combination of water molecules and ethanol molecules in the illustration given earlier, one can tell them apart from each other (at least molecularly) even when they are combined and mixed.

In sum at this juncture: After *the Millennium,* the clockwise spiritual molecules of the Creator are interfaced, admixed, and intermingled with the counter-clockwise spiritual molecules of His entire creation. To be sure, in God's *All-in-all* at the end of *the Millennium,* the two groups of spiritual molecules remain distinguishable from each other even though each group is completely miscible in the other. (Please be reminded that *created beings* never become *the Creator.*)

If the first sentence in the previous paragraph seems too impersonal for a portrait of the intimate relationship between Creator and His created beings, simply replace it with: "After *the Millennium,* the Supreme Being metaphysically embraces His entire creation." Never forget, our Creator-God has emotions and desires. Our Creator-God is not just a force, power, or authority. He is a personal Creator, Savior, and Indweller. It is His love that caused Him to create, save, and re-create us through Christ Jesus. In our love for Him, we should not only worship Him through acts of praise and kindness, we should also fear doing anything that offends Him.

The fear of the LORD is the beginning of wisdom: and the knowledge of the holy is understanding. *Proverbs 9:10 KJV*

Bodies, Somatic Identities, and Forms

In this book, the words *body, somatic identity,* and *form* are used synonymously. *Body* is a common word in English; *somatic identity* comes from the Greek word *soma,* which means *body;* and *form* is a word that is commonly used in philosophy, especially metaphysics, to denote a shape, a structure, or an object. In most cases, the words *body, somatic identity,* and *form* are used for natural, physical, material, or corporeal shapes, structures, and objects. Two primary exceptions exist: (1) when *form* is capitalized in philosophy (i.e., *Form),* then the word refers to the invisible and intangible essence of a physical shape, structure, object, or body. And (2) when *spiritual body* in the Bible is used, it is used in contrast to a natural, physical, material, or corporeal body *(1 Corinthians 15:44 KJV).*

For the present author, the Bible is clear that God the Father and God the Son each have a body, somatic identity, or form. (To be sure, figuratively and metaphysically, they also have a shared *Form.*)

Although God the Holy Spirit is amorphous, God the Father and God the Son each have a body, somatic identity, or form. (Indeed, to be a son, one must look like one's father.) Unfortunately, many people resist the notion that God the Father has a body, somatic identity, or form: (1) partly because of the fiery appearance of the LORD God Almighty presented in the Old Testament; (2) partly because of the fantastic(al) descriptions of the LORD God Almighty in Ezekiel, Isaiah, and Revelation; and (3) partly because of their resistance to the anthropomorphization of Deity.

For the sake of clarity here, "anthropomorphization of Deity" occurs whenever we assign human qualities to God. Most times, the anthropomorphization of Deity makes God too small (that is, with weaknesses, vulnerabilities, and infirmities), just as viewing Deity as only a supernatural force, power, or authority often makes God too big (that is, impersonal, unavailable, and inaccessible). So, we need to be careful not to anthropomorphize God. We should also be careful not to amorphize Him (i.e., conceptualize Him as being without body, somatic identity, or form); the body, somatic identity, and form of God the Father is, of course, an incorporeal body, spiritual somatic identity, and *metaphysical Form.*

The present author prefers the distinction made by Immanuel Kant between *symbolical anthropomorphism* and *dogmatic anthropomorphism.* For Kant, *symbolical anthropomorphism* "concerns language only and not the object itself" *(Prolegomena, p. 106 [1])* in contradistinction to *dogmatic anthropomorphism,* which assigns human characteristics to the Creator-God literally and not figuratively. Thus, using these language labels from Kant, that the Creator-God

---

[1]   Kant, Immanuel. *Prolegomena to any Future Metaphysics Which Will Be Able to Come Forth as Science* (translated from the 1783 edition). New York: The Liberal Arts Press, 1950.

tasted human pain and suffering through the experiences of Christ Jesus represents *symbolical anthropomorphism* and not *dogmatic anthropomorphism.*

If God the Father were amorphous: (1) He would not have been able to walk in the Garden of Eden in the cool of the day *(Genesis 3:8);* (2) He would not have been able to fight physically with Jacob at Peniel *(Genesis 32:24-32);* (3) He would not have been able to show Moses the "hinterparts" (i.e., back parts) of His body, somatic identity, or form *(Exodus 33:18-23);* (4) the Prophet Isaiah would not have been able to see the appearance of the LORD of Hosts *(Isaiah 6:1-9);* (5) the Prophet Ezekiel would not have been able to see "the appearance of the likeness of the glory of the LORD" upon His throne *(Ezekiel 1:26-28);* and (6) the Prophet Daniel would not have been able to describe the appearance of "the Ancient of Days" *(Daniel 7:9-10).*

Although we are able to discern Deity in terms of unfallen man because original man was made in the complete image and perfect likeness of God (as a reflection, or mirror image, of Him), we are not able to as easily work backwards (i.e., regress in our imaginations) from the body, somatic identity, or form of fallen man to the body, somatic identity, or form of God because of an extra inserted step — which step is "the Adamic Fall" itself. Nevertheless, we can still apprehend God the Father's appearance by gaining insight from the Holy Bible.

That our human body, somatic identity, or form resembles God the Father's spiritual body, somatic identity, or form is supported by this reference to "the Ancient of Days" in Chapter Seven of the Book of Daniel:

{9} I beheld until the thrones [or earthly powers] were cast down, and the Ancient of Days did sit, whose garment was white as snow, and the hair of His head like pure wool: His throne was like the fiery flame, and His wheels [or energy vortices] as burning fire. {10} A fiery stream issued and came forth from before Him: millions ministered unto Him, and tens of millions stood before Him: the judgment was set, and the books were opened.[2] [brackets mine] *Daniel 7:9-10 KJV (Paraphrase)*

Although readers or listeners might think (because they have been taught) that verses 9 and 10 are describing the appearance of the Lord Jesus Christ, it is clear that the "Ancient of Days" refers to *God the Father* because "the Son of Man" from verses 13 and 14 of the same chapter of Daniel clearly refers to *God the Son* (who is, of course, Jesus Christ):

{13} I saw visions in the night, and, behold, one like the Son of Man [that is, God the Son] came with the clouds of heaven, and came to the Ancient of Days [that is, God the Father], and they brought him before Him [that is, brought God the Son before God the Father]. {14} And there was given him [God the Son] dominion, and glory, and a kingdom that all people, nations, and languages should serve him [God the Son]: his [God the Son's] dominion is an everlasting dominion, which shall not pass away, and his [God the Son's] kingdom shall not be destroyed.[3] [brackets mine] *Daniel 7:13-14 (Paraphrase)*

Although God is Spirit,[4] whose totality of Being (i.e., His Holy and Fiery Presence) cannot be seen by human beings without their annihilation,[5] God the Father has a body, somatic identity, or form that can step into physicality. *For example*, Jacob fought with God at Peniel when God chose to step into corporeality *(Genesis 32:22-32)*. This, of course, presupposes an appearance at Peniel by God the

---

2   This judgment is the "Great White Throne" Judgment described in Revelation 20:11-15.

3   Compare with Matthew 28:18.

4   John 4:24

5   Exodus 33:20

Father rather than a *theophany* [6] by God the Son. (Obviously, God would have had to *throw the fight* [7] at Peniel in order for Jacob to win.)

The identity of unfallen man included a body, somatic identity, or form — just as the identity of fallen man includes a body, somatic identity, or form. The former was supernatural, spiritual, and incorporeal and understood metaphysically; the latter is natural or corporeal and understood physically. Indeed, the two shapes are different. The shape of fallen man is merely a shadow and iniquitous corruption (i.e., a metaphysical holographic distortion) of the perfect likeness of God that unfallen man originally possessed. The shape of fallen man is three dimensional in a physical universe; the shape of unfallen man was non-dimensional in a spiritual universe. (There are no dimensions in Heaven.)

Concerning God the Father's body, somatic identity, or form, we must seek to understand it metaphysically and not physically. If the reader or listener focuses on God the Father conceptually, then he or she will begin to see His form take shape in the fabric of His spiritual universe. Neither phantasm nor phantom, God the Father has an incorporeal body, somatic identity, or form just as He has an essence, or *Form.*

To be sure, God the Father has also shown Himself to human beings through His only-begotten Son, Jesus Christ — especially through his works:

Jesus said unto him: "Have I been with you so long, and yet have you not known me, Philip? If he who has seen me has seen the Father, why would you say: 'Show us the Father?'" *John 14:9 KJV (Paraphrase)*

---

[6] "Theophany" generally refers to an appearance by the pre-incarnate Christ during Old Testament times.

[7] "Throw the fight" is an English idiom that means "lose on purpose."

John 14:9 means that anyone who recognized and knew God the Son also recognized and knew God the Father.

Astral Gelatinous™

The phrase *astral gelatinous*™ was coined by the present author and first copyrighted in the 2011 edition of his book entitled *Divine Metaphysics of Human Anatomy* (United States Copyright Office TXu001788674). Simply stated, the phrase represents spiritual living substance, which, if seen by human beings, would appear semisolid and translucent.

The phrase *astral gelatinous*™ describes a substance that predominantly has spiritual qualities similar to the created substance of unfallen angels. This substance may also take on physical qualities depending on the dimensionality in which it is found or into which it has been projected. *For example,* when some angels step into the physical realm (i.e., *push* themselves into our relative space-time), they voluntarily take on human form and appear to be human even though they did not originate from, or in, a hominin life form. This is exemplified by the angels who first visited Abraham and, later, Lot in the city of Sodom — which visitations are recorded in Chapters Eighteen and Nineteen of the Book of Genesis. At one time, certain angels even stepped into physicality in order to have sexual intercourse with human beings. This sexual interaction is recorded in Genesis 6:1-4 as having taken place between "the sons of God" and "the daughters of men." The giants, or *nephilim* (i.e., "fallen ones"), mentioned in Genesis 6:4 and Numbers 13:33 of the Holy Bible were the offspring of these unnatural sexual liaisons. The Holy Bible is clear that the spiritual beings who mated with human beings are now relegated to the *bottomless pit of the Abyss in Hades,* awaiting the Creator-Savior's final judgment and condemnation for their eternally-cursed transgression (see verse 6 of the Epistle of Jude).

From the present author's perspective, the unfallen creation that originally reflected the Creator-Savior's complete image and perfect likeness (as a reflection, or mirror-image, of Him) was *astral gelatinous™* in spiritual nature, substance, and essence. As a result of the Adamic Fall, the *astral gelatinous™* substance of immortal beings, originally created in the complete image and perfect likeness of the Creator-Savior, manifested as living physical substance (i.e., protoplasm). Consequently, the various cells, tissues, organs, and organ systems of the modern hominin appeared, becoming mere representations, vestiges, remnants, and "fossilized impressions" of what they used to be. In other words, when the fallen Adam and Eve were expelled from the Garden of Eden, they materialized as human beings and appeared alongside other human beings who had evolved on Earth without souls. (*For example,* like other primates living at the time, Neanderthal men and women did not possess eternal souls.)

As mentioned earlier, at the return of Christ Jesus, all who are joint heirs with him shall receive their new somatic identities. These new somatic identities not only resemble the body of the ascended Christ Jesus *(1 John 3:2 KJV)* but also are composed of the same *astral gelatinous™* substance that constituted the somatic identities of immortal beings before the Adamic Fall.

At the time of the Adamic Fall, immortal beings became mortal beings. Mortal beings only become re-immortalized by believing on the efficacy of the shed blood of Jesus Christ.

In sum at this juncture, *astral gelatinous™* substance is the spiritual substance of immortal beings. It has spiritually-translucent, spiritually-luminescent, and spiritually-iridescent qualities that reflect the *glory,* or spiritual light, of the Creator-Savior. *Astral gelatinous™* substance is metaphysically light, airy, and glowy.

For the sake of clarity, gender and sexual identity do not exist in an *astral gelatinous™* condition of being. Instead, beneficial mental and emotional characteristics associated with each gender and sexual identity on Earth are fused together for each entity in Heaven.

In short, there are no males, females, hermaphrodites, or intersexuals in Heaven. All beings in Heaven are spiritual, not physical.

In the *first resurrection,* as Jesus Christ returns to the Earth at the beginning of *the Millennium,* the souls of all saved dead human beings and all saved living human beings will receive their new spiritualized somatic identities (i.e., *astral gelatinous™* forms, not *physical protoplasmic* forms). In the *second resurrection,* when all physical forms will cease to exist at the end of *the Millennium* (in fulfillment of 1 Corinthians 15:28 and 2 Peter 3:10-12 KJV), all remaining souls who have committed their obeisance and fealty to Jesus Christ during *the Millennium* will receive their new spiritualized somatic identities. It is at this time that the Creator-God will be *All-in-all.*

On Repentance and Forgiveness

If you, the reader or listener, desire salvation, I invite you to believe in your heart and confess with your mouth by repeating the following prayer out loud:

Dear Heavenly Father, I ask that you forgive me of my sins. I am sorry for them and I repent of them. I accept your only-begotten Son, Jesus Christ, as my Lord and Savior. I know that Jesus Christ is the only-begotten Son of the one true and only real Creator-God, the God of the Holy Bible. I invite You (God the Father and God the Son) into my soul, my heart, and my mind, and I ask that You help me to live for You each day. Thank You for hearing my prayer in the Name of Jesus Christ. Thank You for accepting me as one of Your own. And thank You for cleansing me of all of my sins by his shed blood. Dear Creator-God, help me to trust in You alone throughout the rest of my earthly life.

On Daily Prayer Requests

Extrapolated from the Bible, one formula (i.e., template) for daily prayer includes asking God the Father in the name of God the Son at the same time that we anticipate in faith that our prayer request(s) will be answered through the agency of God the Holy Spirit (but answered only in accordance with the Godhead's Will).

In other words, we might begin each daily prayer with *"Dear Heavenly Father, in the name of Jesus Christ, I (we) ask that ..."* and end each prayer with *"Thank you for hearing and answering my (our) prayer for Thy Name's sake."*

Afterword

In order for Christians to fully comprehend the true nature, substance, and essence of the Godhead: (1) they should be willing to conceptually hold His unity *(His Oneness)* as they simultaneously attend to His individual parts *(His Threeness);* and (2) they should be willing to accept that His individual parts *(God the Father, God the Son,* and *God the Holy Spirit)* are simultaneous and synchronous and not only sequential.

It is the present author's opinion that *Oneness Christians* staunchly believe in their *Oneness* doctrines either (1) because they were indoctrinated in those doctrines from an early age and never questioned their accuracy in describing the Godhead or (2) because *Threeness* doctrines are more difficult to cognitively assimilate and accommodate. *For example,* just as it is easier to juggle one ball than two balls, and just as it is easier to juggle two balls than three balls, so is it easier to conceptualize God's *Being* in one person rather than God's *Being* in two persons, and so is it easier to conceptualize God's *Being* in two persons rather than God's *Being* in three persons.

The present author believes that a fair and impartial re-reading of all verses in the Bible will help *Oneness* adherents fully grasp the simultaneous and synchronous *Threeness* of God.

Books by the Author

As I See It: The Nature of Reality by God by Rev. Joseph Adam Pearson, Ph.D., Christ Evangelical Bible Institute, Copyright 2022. ISBN 978-0615590615.

Classroom Version of As I See It: The Nature of Reality by God by Rev. Joseph Adam Pearson, Ph.D., Christ Evangelical Bible Institute, Copyright 2022. ISBN-13: 978-1734294705.

God, Our Universal Self: A Primer for Future Christian Metaphysics by Rev. Joseph Adam Pearson, Ph.D., Christ Evangelical Bible Institute, Copyright 2022. ISBN 978-0985772857.

Divine Metaphysics of Human Anatomy by Rev. Joseph Adam Pearson, Ph.D., Christ Evangelical Bible Institute, Copyright 2022. ISBN 978-0985772819.

Hello from 3050 AD! by Rev. Joseph Adam Pearson, Ph.D., Christ Evangelical Bible Institute, Copyright 2023 ISBN 978-0996222402.

Christianity and Homosexuality Reconciled: New Thinking for a New Millennium! by Rev. Joseph Adam Pearson, Ph.D., Christ Evangelical Bible Institute, Copyright 2021. ISBN 978-0985772888.

The Koran (al-Qur'an): Testimony of Antichrist by Rev. Joseph Adam Pearson, Ph.D., Christ Evangelical Bible Institute, Copyright 2020. ISBN 978-0985772833.

Telugu Version of Quran: Testimony of Antichrist by Rev. Joseph Adam Pearson, Ph.D., Christ Evangelical Bible Institute, Copyright 2020. ISBN 978-0996222457.

Urdu Version of Quran: Testimony of Antichrist by Rev. Joseph Adam Pearson, Ph.D., Christ Evangelical Bible Institute, Copyright 2020. ISBN 978-0996222440.

Revelation of Antichrist by Rev. Joseph Adam Pearson, Ph.D., Christ Evangelical Bible Institute, Copyright 2021. ISBN 9780996222488.

Intelligent Evolution by Rev. Joseph Adam Pearson, Ph.D., Christ Evangelical Bible Institute, Copyright 2022. ISBN 978-0996222426.

The Biology of Psychism from a Christian Perspective by Rev. Joseph Adam Pearson, Ph.D., Christ Evangelical Bible Institute, Copyright 2020. ISBN 978-0996222464.

The Threeness of God by Rev. Joseph Adam Pearson, Ph.D., Christ Evangelical Bible Institute, Copyright 2023. ISBN 978-1734294729.

To access free pdf editions of Dr. Pearson's books, visit:

http://www.christevangelicalbibleinstitute.com

or

http://www.dr-joseph-adam-pearson.com

About the Author

Dr. Joseph Adam Pearson is a college and university educator with more than fifty years of classroom and administrative experience. Dr. Pearson has been the International President and Chief Executive Officer of Christ Evangelical Bible Institute (CEBI) for over twenty-five years. At the time of the latest publication of this book (2023), he still oversees thriving branch campuses of CEBI in India, Pakistan, and Tanzania.

Currently, Dr. Pearson spends the majority of his time developing, designing, and deploying curriculum for Christian education nationally and internationally. And he preaches, teaches, and leads international crusades as well as provides group pastoral training in global mission settings.

During his professional life, Dr. Pearson has also served in the role of Senior Pastor of Healing Waters Ministries in Tempe, Arizona and as Dean of Instruction for Mesa Community College in Mesa, Arizona — where he was founding instructional dean for its Red Mountain Campus as well as Director of its Extended Campus.

Dr. Pearson holds a Bachelor of Science degree in Biology from Loyola University (Chicago), a Master of Science degree in Biology from Loyola University (Chicago), and a Ph.D. in Curriculum and Instruction with specializations in language, literacy, linguistics, and textual analysis from Arizona State University. He has also taken additional doctoral level coursework at the University of Chicago and at the University of Illinois Medical Center.

Dr. Pearson believes that after we are saved, and at the same time we are being sanctified, our individual lives and deeds are part of an "application" for the jobs that we will each hold during Christ Jesus' Millennial reign on Earth. Dr. Pearson's greatest goal is to be one of the many committed Christian educators who will be teaching during that period of time.

You may contact Dr. Pearson at drjpearson@aol.com or drjosephadampearson@gmail.com

www.ingramcontent.com/pod-product-compliance
Lightning Source LLC
Chambersburg PA
CBHW081221020426
42331CB00012B/3066